AF352242

Kalamazoo
County

"Kalamazoo County's Enterprises"
by Peter Schmitt

Produced in cooperation with the
Kalamazoo County Chamber of Commerce

Windsor Publications, Inc.
Chatsworth, California

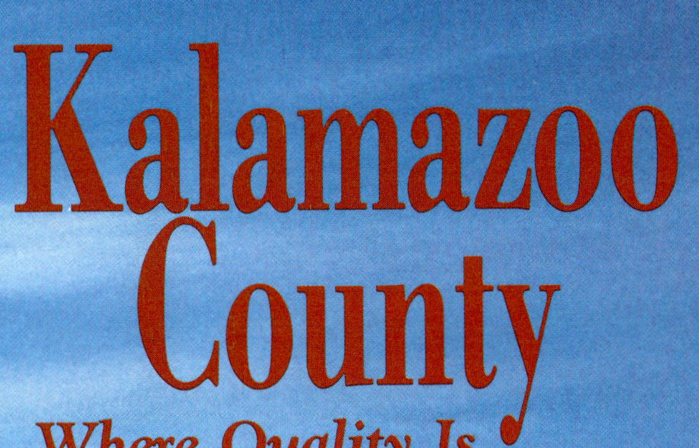

Kalamazoo
County
Where Quality Is
a Way of Life
A Contemporary Portrait
by Fred McTaggart

Windsor Publications, Inc.—
History Books Division
Managing Editor: Karen Story
Design Director: Alexander D'Anca

Staff for *Kalamazoo County*
Manuscript Editor: Doreen Nakakihara
Photo Editor: Larry Molmud
Senior Editor, Corporate Profiles: Judith L. Hunter
Senior Production Editor, Corporate Profiles: Phyllis Gray
Customer Service Manager: Phyllis Feldman- Schroeder
Editorial Consultant: Barbara L. Menlen
Editorial Assistants: Kim Kievman, Michael Nugwynne, Kathy B.
   Peyser, Theresa J. Solis
Publisher's Representatives, Corporate Profiles: John Swedberg,
   Lisa Swedberg
Layout Artist, Corporate Profiles: Mari Catherine Preimesberger
Designer: Christina L. Rosepapa

Library of Congress Cataloging-in-Publication Data
McTaggart, Fred.
   Kalamazoo County : where quality is a way of life : a contemporary portrait / by Fred McTaggart ; Kalamazoo County's enterprises by Peter Schmitt ; produced in cooperation with the Kalamazoo County Chamber of Commerce. — 1st ed.
   p. 144 cm. 23 x 31
   Bibliography: p. 141
   Includes index.
   ISBN 0-89781-268-9 : $29.95
   1. Kalamazoo County (Mich.)—Economic conditions. 2. Quality of life—Michigan—Kalamazoo County. I. Kalamazoo County Chamber of Commerce (Kalamazoo County, Mich.) II. Title.
HC107.M52K355 1989
306'.09774'17—dc20 89-32455   CIP

Windsor Publications, Inc.
Elliot Martin, Chairman of the Board
James L. Fish III, Chief Operating Officer
Michele Sylvestro, Vice President/Sales-Marketing

Previous spread: Swimmers take a stroll along a jetty on Lake Michigan. Photo by Patricia A. Bulthuis

Contents

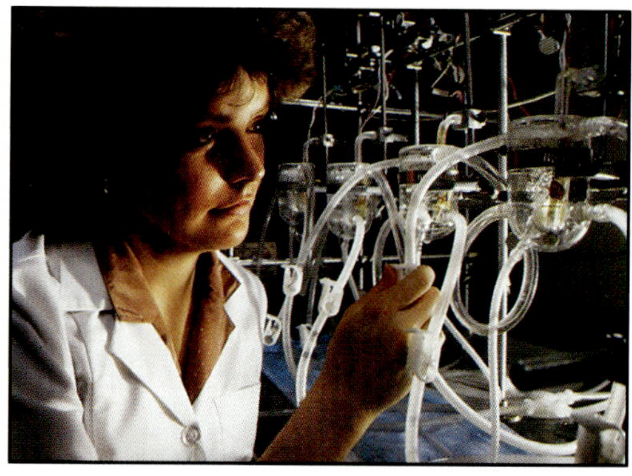

Northbound traffic winds its way downtown along Westnedge Avenue at dusk. Photo by John D. Strauss

Prologue

In Kalamazoo County, as in other communities across America, there is one significant challenge, one that literally means life or death for our community: we must have economic growth and prosperity in order to better our way of living.

The world is constantly changing as it heads into a new century. Such change is a sign that the human spirit never gives up on finding better ways to get the job done. The Kalamazoo County Chamber of Commerce never stops at finding better ways to get the job done, either. Since its beginning 85 years ago, its responsibility has grown as the organization leading Kalamazoo County to excellence.

During its first few years, the chamber of commerce focused on all the services so necessary in a small community. It helped establish a community foundation and started a fund for needy people that today is the Greater Kalamazoo United Way. The chamber helped set up a traffic system and establish roads to neighboring communities to increase the flow of commerce.

Today the community is much larger; its needs are larger, too. Because it helped build such a strong foundation decades ago, the chamber can now face other emerging issues—issues like forming a more cohesive way to run area governments, bettering the education and career opportunities for local children, providing tools and advocacy so business can grow and prosper, and attracting new tourist and convention dollars.

The Kalamazoo County Chamber of Commerce and its participating member firms are underwriting the publication of *Kalamazoo County: Where Quality Is a Way of Life* to celebrate the community's rich diversity, current economic growth, and vibrancy. In this book businesses, industries, community organizations, health care facilities, and educators describe their contributions to Kalamazoo County's history, current vitality, and future development. Sponsorship of this publication is another example of the organization's commitment to Kalamazoo County—its pride in it—and its hope for it.

Kalamazoo County: Where Quality Is a Way of Life will provide an interesting, enjoyable look at the key players who shape Kalamazoo County. The chamber gladly accepts a leading role in this flourishing community. It is proud to have helped build the foundation for a forward-thinking community of like-minded citizens continuing the progress of the past into a dynamic future.

J. Michael Kemp
Chairman of the Board
Kalamazoo County Chamber of Commerce

A candy cane walk makes a
fanciful setting for this elfin visitor to Bronson Park at Christmas-

Foreword

by Blaine Lam

Who among us has not been asked to characterize the community in which we live? Those of us who reside in Kalamazoo County find it difficult to provide a single, completely adequate response. Just as the rivers, prairies, and magnificent tree stands converge to provide our natural setting; just as our seasons rotate; and even as the day and night replace each other—so do our images of life in Kalamazoo County blend, then turn and, at times, completely change.

The human dynamics here have really been something, and from Fred McTaggart's work, *Kalamazoo County: Where Quality Is a Way of Life,* we gain a more complete appreciation for those dynamics and for the diversity that so enriches our history.

Interestingly, the way we hear many Kalamazoo County residents characterize our community's greatest strength is in terms of its diversity. The diversity of our economy, for instance, has at times helped us forestall recession. Our ethnic and cultural diversity is celebrated in fairs and festivals, but more importantly provides us with the melting-pot heritage that promotes a daily, personal understanding of the larger world.

As our greatest strength, diversity, it seems, also contains the seeds of our greatest failures—differences that could not be reconciled. Kalamazoo County has not escaped the political, racial, economic, educational, and social differences that so many times have stood between us and greater accomplishments. As a community, we have suffered through our share of strife and pain, some constructive and some senseless.

By fair comparative standards, of course, Kalamazoo County would have to stand out as a successful community. What strikes you in reading McTaggart's work, however, is that so many of the men and women who shaped our institutions, who shaped our community life,

were not in pursuit of comparative excellence. They were in pursuit of quality.

Those of us familiar with the philosophy of the late Dr. W.E. Upjohn instantly recognize the significance of the word "quality" in connection with a book about our community. A century ago, the doctor proclaimed that his workers should "keep the quality up." Great concept. For a company. For a community. This book reveals, of course, that while The Upjohn Company certainly had no lock on the concept, its leaders—particularly W.E. Upjohn—were willing to nourish and support community efforts that contributed to the quality of life.

There has been an unmistakable spirit—call it community spirit, or simply community—abiding among the residents of Kalamazoo County these past 150-plus years. We keep it alive, in part, by telling the stories of our pioneers, of our leaders, of the many changes and challenges we've faced and, yes, even of our difficulties.

McTaggart's work shows us just how committed our commerce leaders have been to the governmental, cultural, and educational programs and institutions within the community. At the same time, the men and women who have run our governmental, cultural, and educational programs and institutions have remained responsive to community needs and desires. The overlapping and intertwining of public and private lives in Kalamazoo County don't show up by coincidence, of course. We see an underlying understanding of what community is all about, and what it takes to "keep the quality of life up."

A text of this nature necessarily falls short in identifying all the people, all the businesses, and all the organizations that have helped shape the community. That's less a failing of McTaggart or any other writer than a tribute to how much has been accomplished in our community.

If you know and love this community, any portrait is incomplete. One moment, you've got a glimpse of what all this must have looked like to Titus Bronson and his contemporaries. Then, you catch a vision of the things that can be done in the next 5 or 10 years. Finally,

you return to the reality that contains both triumph and struggle, conflict and compromise, diversity that enriches and differences that divide.

Ideally, a book such as this helps our sense of community materialize. It places the complexities of our modern, more urban setting against a simpler, historical backdrop, providing us with something of a stopping point that defines the scope and scale of our community. Roots that many of us knew were there are retraced in this book. New insights are offered. New perspectives are brought to light. New tidbits of information are sprinkled throughout.

This book, quite frankly, has a positive slant. Because it was written in cooperation with the Kalamazoo County Chamber of Commerce, that comes as neither a surprise nor a drawback. The chamber has been one of those community organizations historically on the lookout for the positive, the constructive, the new, and the progressive.

Such an approach doesn't have to ignore or negate the difficulties that face us as a community as we continue to pursue quality in the way we live with each other, and the way we coexist with those in our region, other parts of the country, and the rest of the world.

Indeed, our most successful citizens have volunteered to tackle our most serious problems head on. Quite often, however, they have used disagreement to forge consensus. These leaders have understood conflict as a means of achieving cooperation.

In recent years throughout Kalamazoo County, we've heard a great deal about the need for a new spirit of unity, which—when you think about it—is the last word in community. There's no misreading Kalamazoo County's tremendous potential, the realization of which is up to those who choose to stay here or move here. Unity, in light of the many differences, may be impossible. Harmony, however, in light of our great diversity, should be achievable. You can hear the strains of harmony—people of vastly different backgrounds, working with a sense of community—throughout this work.

The result has been quality. Let's keep it up.

Part

1

City Life, Country Pleasures

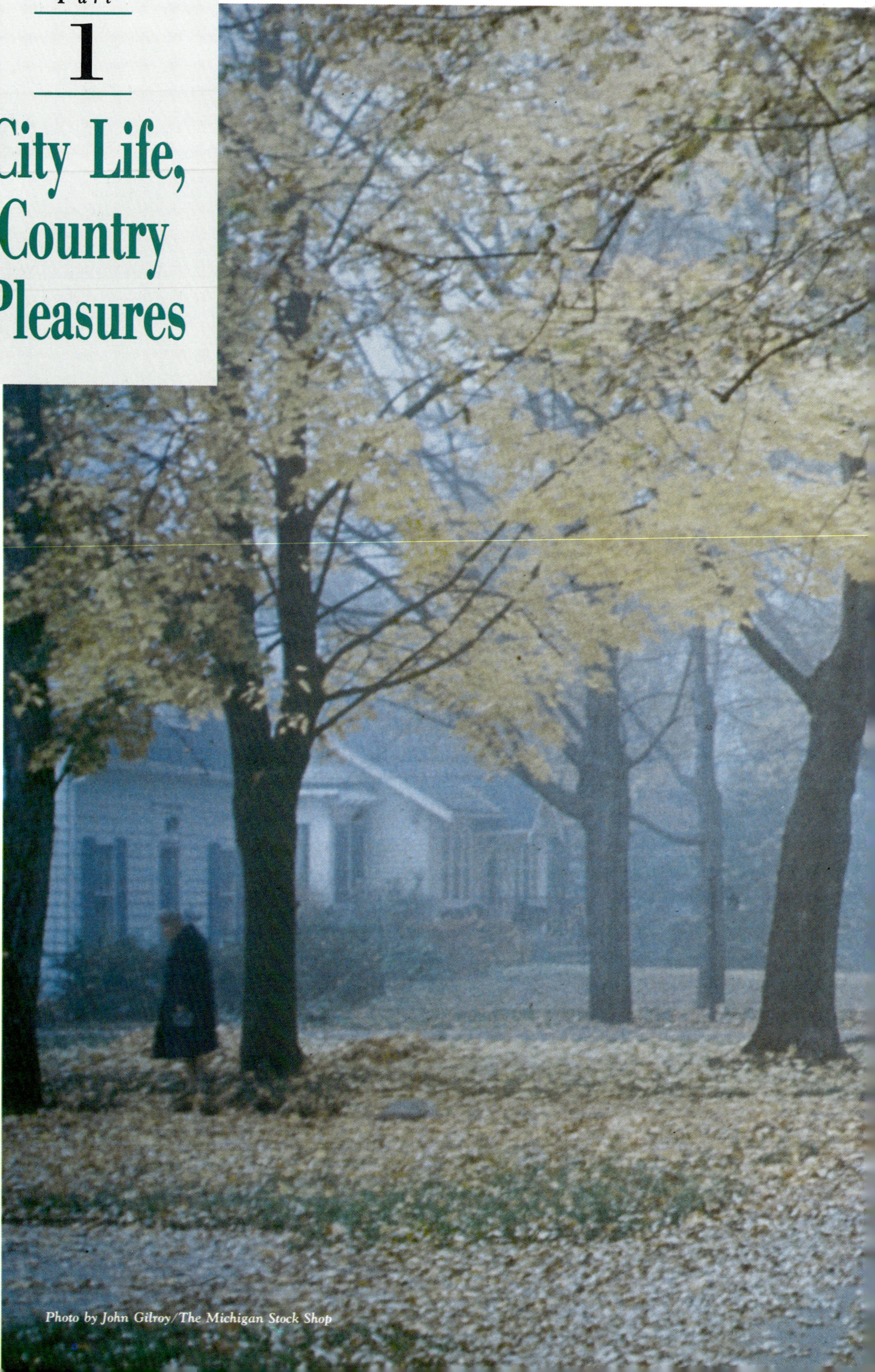

A Good Place to Live and Do Business

Citizens took to the streets to celebrate the nation's centennial on July 4, 1876. For a town not yet 50 years old, Kalamazoo presented a strikingly sophisticated urban image. Courtesy, The Michigan Stock Shop

When the French explorer La Salle visited southwest Michigan, he wrote with awe of the great meadows covered with "rank grass." On March 28, 1680, his journal reports, he stopped on the border of the largest of these prairies, Prairie Ronde, near what is now Schoolcraft. La Salle's party spent the day shooting the plentiful game—deer, bears, squirrels, rabbits, raccoons, wild turkeys, quails, partridges, pheasants, passenger pigeons, and enormous flocks of ducks and geese. Then they rested on what an early writer described as a "broad and beautiful savanna, covered, at that date . . . with a vesture of flowers that gave it almost fairy-like beauty."

Compared to the massive prairies found at that time in Illinois and Iowa, those of southwest Michigan were small islands amid the heavy timber that included several varieties of oak and hickory, elm, beech, maple, basswood, black walnut, butternut, black cherry, ash, sycamore, sour gum, birch, larch, and cedar. Figuring prominently in the varied landscape were "oak openings"— level areas loosely timbered with towering burr oak trees, creating what resembled a large forested auditorium. Bronson Park in downtown Kalamazoo was once a fine example of an oak opening, and many of the features remain there and at Pioneer Park (South Westnedge Street and Park Place) near downtown Kalamazoo.

The Potawatomi Indians who lived in the area at that time knew it was a good place to live. The land was fertile, yielding a good supply of corn, pumpkins, squash, beans, and gourds. It was dotted with lakes and ponds, tucked away neatly in the gently rolling landscape. Drinking water was always available, and fish and game were abundant. Probably most important, to the Potawatomi, were the rivers and streams flowing through the area and eventually leading to the "great water" of Lake Michigan. In their view, these were "the source of life" and "the arteries and veins of our Grandmother, the earth."

The name Kalamazoo comes from a Potawatomi word signifying the way water bubbles up from the bottom of the Kalamazoo River. To the Potawatomi this was a special place, and to the early settlers—for somewhat different reasons—it was clearly a good place to settle and make a home.

The city of Kalamazoo is located at the convergence of four major Indian trails, near the shallows of the Kalamazoo River. Major Indian villages at that time were located in Ypsilanti, Ann Arbor, Battle Creek, Gull Prairie, Kalamazoo, Schoolcraft, South Haven, and St. Joseph—connected by rivers and streams in addition to well-traveled land trails.

During the War of 1812, this area was considered a safe retreat for Potawatomi women and children. The British set up a blacksmith forge near what is now Kleinstuck Preserve to repair weapons used by the Indians in the war against the Americans. Soon afterward the American Fur Company built a trading post on the great bend of the Kalamazoo River, near what is now Riverside Cemetery. These were the earliest records of white men in the area, but the land was still virtually untamed when the first settlers started to arrive.

Pioneering Kalamazoo County

Bazel Harrison and his wife, Martha, left Ohio on September 20, 1828, with their 6 children and 13 friends and relatives. They were on their way to the new land of Michigan, riding in a long Pennsylvania wagon. It was painted bright blue, packed with possessions, and drawn by a team of horses. It was followed by four smaller "Ohio" wagons, drawn by oxen, and a single-horse wagon in which Martha Harrison and her daughters slept. They brought 3 cows, 50 head of sheep, and 50 hogs.

The journey was slow. Once they spent seven days going around a swamp that lay in their path. When they camped at night, building a watch fire to keep wolves and other animals away, they quite often could see the smoke rising from the embers of the campfire they had left that morning.

When they passed Elkhart Prairie in Indiana, several members of the party wanted to settle there, but Harrison had his heart set on the new territory in Michigan. Indians along the way confirmed his belief that the great Round Prairie was only about 40 miles to the north.

Finally, as the sun was setting on November 5, 1828, they reached the edge of Prairie Ronde. Chief Sagemaw and 12 of his Potawatomi, in ceremonial dress, greeted them as if they were long-lost brothers and showered them with gifts as well as information about the land. When Harrison signed to the Potawatomi that he wished to settle near water, they guided him to the shores of what would later be named Harrison's Lake, three miles east of Schoolcraft.

In the next weeks 50 to 60 settlers followed Harrison to Prairie Ronde including John Vickers, who later moved several miles east to open a gristmill on Portage Creek near what is now Vicksburg. All of these settlers gathered a year later, pitching in to help Titus Bronson—a potato farmer from Ann Arbor—erect his log cabin. Historians say this cabin was located at what is now the corner of Church and Water streets.

Though eccentric and controversial, Titus Bronson was a shrewd man who recognized the commercial potential of a place so well situated and endowed with natural assets. He purchased 160 acres on his carefully chosen site, platted a village, successfully campaigned to have it selected as the county seat, then deliberately went about attracting the commercial and industrial elements that would make it prosper. As Bronson prophesied to an early skeptic: "In 20 years from this time you will see a large city here, and you will be able to go to and from Detroit in one day by railroad cars."

In the years between 1829 and 1833, the other townships of the county were settled in rapid succession: Comstock in the fall of 1829 by William Toland; Climax by Caleb Eldred in 1831; Oshtemo by Benjamin Drake in 1829, closely followed by Enoch Harris, the first black settler in the county; Portage by a man named Herring in 1830; Richland and Gull Prairie in May 1830 by Colonel Isaac Barnes; and Ross and Charleston in 1831.

These settlers were interested in the fertile farmland on the prairies but, like Titus Bronson, they also envisioned thriving commercial centers. Enterprising individuals platted towns and cities that grew quickly. Until 1835 Schoolcraft was the largest and most flourishing community in the county. The village of Comstock was a vigorous contender for county seat; if it had won, it might well have become a major commercial and industrial center.

Building Commerce and Industry

The railroad that Titus Bronson foresaw arrived in 1846, and it was an important factor in the development of the area. Yet it certainly was no more important than the two rivers that were so vital to those who lived on the land before the coming of the white man. Even though the pioneers migrated over land to Kalamazoo County, they quickly began to make use of the Kalamazoo and St. Joseph rivers to move goods to market and bring back consumer items for sale.

David S. Walbridge, who moved to Kalamazoo from Buffalo, New York, formed a company to build and operate flatboats on the Kalamazoo River. Boats were loaded with flour, grain, fruits, and vegetables at the mouth of Portage Creek for a three-day trip to the mouth of the river on Lake Mich-

Above: One of Kalamazoo's most famous enterprises, Gibson Guitar Manufacturing Company has brought music to the hands of millions, from amateurs to superstars like B.B. King. Courtesy, The Michigan Stock Shop

Left: Kalamazoo's founder, potato farmer Titus Bronson, made his home where Church and Water streets now meet. Courtesy, The Michigan Stock Shop

igan, then returned to Kalamazoo.

From the beginning the rivers and streams provided an indispensable source of power. Sawmills and gristmills were constructed in Kalamazoo, Augusta, Galesburg, Comstock, and Portage. For many years after the arrival of the early settlers, the gentle current and constant volume of the Kalamazoo River and its tributaries powered more than 50 percent of local industry. Abundant water, as well as waterpower, was an important factor in the development of the paper industry—the county's most important industry around the turn of the century.

In the early days industrial development in Kalamazoo County centered on agricultural products and goods for local consumption: milling grain, processing flour, and manufacturing carriages, buggies, wagons, agricultural implements, concrete, lumber, and building materials. With the founding of the Kalamazoo Paper Company, the Bryant mill, the Bardeen Paper Company in Otsego, the Lee Paper Company in Vicksburg, and the Kalamazoo Vegetable Parchment Company in Parchment, Kalamazoo County became a major center for the manufacture of paper. By World War I it

was the largest paper-producing area in the United States. The paper industry is still an important element in Parchment, Vicksburg, Plainwell, and Kalamazoo.

Through the years a number of products originating in Kalamazoo County made their way into the hands and hearts of the nation. Calvin Forbes, a graduate of Parsons Business College and the son of a building contractor, formed the Kalamazoo Handle Manufacturing Company and set about putting "Kalamazoo Croquet" sets in homes throughout the country and the world—including a permanent court on the lawn of the county courthouse.

Blues musician B.B. King is proud of his guitar that for years was made to his specifications at the Gibson Guitar Manufacturing Company in Kalamazoo. Checker Cabs that roam the streets of America have been assembled or built from parts manufactured at Checker Motors. Other businesses included the Kalamazoo Brewing Company, the Kalamazoo Cigar Company, the Kazoo Suspender Company ("it holds up the pants and the stockings too"), and the Kalamazoo Corset Company—the largest corset-manufacturing company in the world during the 1890s, employing more than 800,

Above right: W.E. Upjohn, M.D., together with his brothers Henry, Frederick, and James, founded the Upjohn Pill and Granule Company in 1885. Today, The Upjohn Company is the area's largest employer. Courtesy, The Michigan Stock Shop

Right: The Kalamazoo Corset Company was the largest maker of corsets in the world during the 1890s and employed more than 800 workers. Courtesy, The Michigan Stock Shop

mostly women. Arthur J. Patterson, manager of Beecher and Kymer's Bookstore, devised the rules for the card game "Flinch" — one of the most popular parlor games in the first half of the twentieth century. He and others then formed the Flinch Card Company to manufacture and distribute the cards. The Kalamazoo Stove Company warmed America with ranges, cookstoves, and heaters, "From Kalamazoo Direct To You."

In 1883 William E. Upjohn, M.D., of Hastings, Michigan, patented the "friable pill" process. Two years later, with his brothers Henry, Frederick, and James, he founded the Upjohn Pill and Granule Company. Today a *Fortune* 500 company, The Upjohn Company is the area's largest employer. In the twentieth century another physician—orthopedic surgeon Homer B. Stryker, M.D.—patented a number of important medical innovations including a rubber heel for leg and foot casts, a frame for turning patients with spinal injuries, an over-the-bed frame to support limbs in traction, a grasping bar to enable patients to move themselves in bed, a hip nailing board, and an oscillating saw to cut casts without injuring underlying flesh. With the formation of the Stryker Corporation in 1946, health care became a major industry in Kalamazoo County.

While agriculture has always played a key role in the area, industrial and economic development have exhibited great diversity. In recent years the health care and paper industries have continued to thrive, along with automotive products, chemicals and plastics, aircraft and missiles, foods, and banking.

Since the early days, Kalamazoo County residents have recognized the need for good public services to provide heat, light, and water for their homes and factories. The Kalamazoo Gas Light Company, established in 1855, manufactured gas from coal. It built and maintained 15 miles of gas lines for residential customers, producing more illuminating gas than any company outside of Detroit and Grand Rapids.

Soon after the Civil War, Kalamazoo became one of the first communities in the state to develop a sophisticated city water system. Through three separate bond issues of $25,000 each, a deep well was sunk, a steam pumping system was installed to bring in water from springs, and more than 15 miles of water pipe were laid in the village. A waterworks building was constructed on Burdick Street, and a water commissioner was hired to supervise the system.

The first drainage sewer was laid in 1851, and in 1881 the village charter was amended to provide for a board of sewerage commissioners and the construction of sanitary sewers. Highly advanced for its time, this system could separate sanitary from storm water drainage and eliminated the handling of storm water through the water reclamation plant. It served the community well, and became integrated into a state-of-the-art water reclamation system in the mid-1980s.

When Dorothea Dix focused public attention on the plight of the mentally ill in the mid-1800s, Michigan became one of the first states to establish a state mental institution. The citizens of Kalamazoo donated $1,500 plus land for this purpose, convincing the state to locate the institution in Kalamazoo. Opened in 1859, the first mental institution in the state is now known as the Kalamazoo Regional Psychiatric Hospital.

By tradition, the physically ill were still cared for at home. It was not until 1889 that a St. Augustine parish priest, Father Francis O'Brien, summoned 11 Sisters of St. Joseph from Watertown, New York, to open the county's first hospital: Borgess Medical Center. Fifty-nine patients were treated in 1890, but by the turn of the century the hospital had provided care for more than 233 patients. This required the construction of

Above: Kalamazoo's diverse economy has historically remained stable while others have plummeted. This bustling 1938 street scene shows little sign of the Great Depression that was ravaging much of the country. Courtesy, The Michigan Stock Shop

Above: Another early Kalamazoo business was Checker Motors, builders of parts for the nation's familiar Checker Cabs. Courtesy, The Michigan Stock Shop

A History of Refinement

In the nineteenth century—as today—life was good in Kalamazoo. Jobs were available close to home but without the complexities of city life. Enterprising individuals had ample opportunity to act out the American Dream. Local shops offered an excellent assortment of consumer items as well as fresh fruits and vegetables. Then, as now, residents of Kalamazoo County had abundant opportunities for intellectual growth.

The cultural bent of the county was established very early. The first high school was established in 1858, and a landmark decision of the Michigan Supreme Court (the Kalamazoo School Case, 1874) upheld the rights of communities to levy taxes for public high schools. From the early days Kalamazoo County residents were proud of their educational facilities. In 1833 the Michigan legislature incorporated a school under the name of the Michigan and Huron Institute and in 1836 classes began in a two-story frame building on Cedar Street between Park and Westnedge. Renamed the Kalamazoo Literary Institute in 1837, it was the beginning of Kalamazoo College, now a highly respected liberal arts institution. During the 1850s enrollment at Kalamazoo College and its Baptist Theological Seminary was about 400—more than double that of the University of Michigan's School of Literature, Science, and the Arts.

new wings on the converted mansion, located on the 300 block of Portage Street. Later a new hospital was built on Gull Road.

In 1900 a handful of local physicians and businesspersons organized to construct a hospital that later became affiliated with the Methodist church and was named Bronson Methodist Hospital. Today both Kalamazoo hospitals are major regional medical centers, with complementary areas of specialization. Together they employ more than 5,000 persons, truly making Kalamazoo a health care county.

Victorian Kalamazooans cultivate their minds with the help of the city's fine public library facilities in this photograph taken around 1890. Courtesy, The Michigan Stock Shop

In 1838—three years before the establishment of its main campus at Ann Arbor—the University of Michigan set up branch campuses throughout the state, including one in a frame building in Bronson Park in Kalamazoo. After a few years funding for the "Old Branch" was discontinued, but until that time the community had two institutions of higher learning, setting a precedent that has been maintained through most of the county's history.

Starting in 1867 the Michigan Female Seminary provided two years of higher education for women. With the founding in 1903 of Western State Normal School (which later would become Western Michigan University), the Michigan Female Seminary faced declining enrollment and finally closed its doors in 1907. Today, however, the county boasts three four-year institutions, a business college, and a community college.

Meanwhile Parsons Business College, established in 1869, attracted students from throughout the area including W.K. Kellogg of Battle Creek. His signature (undoubtedly influenced by the penmanship made famous at Parsons) is now inscribed on thousands of cereal boxes around the world.

The *Kalamazoo Gazette* (originally the *Michigan Statesman*) was established in 1835, the first newspaper in the state outside of Detroit. From 1846 to 1862 the editor and publisher of the *Gazette* was Volney Haskall, who was also an attorney, a graduate of the Kalamazoo Literary Institute, and a gifted thinker. Political debate between the Democratic *Gazette* and the Whig newspaper, the *Telegraph*, was waged vigorously and on a high intellectual plane.

The *Telegraph* is thought to be the first Michigan publication to have advocated the formation of a third party, the Republican party. In 1856 Abraham Lincoln spoke in support of the candidacy of John C. Fremont at a huge, statewide Republican rally in Bronson Park. Four years later, when Lincoln was himself the candidate, Kalamazoo County gave him a resounding edge over Stephen Douglas by a ratio of 3-to-2.

The Kalamazoo Lyceum was formed as early as 1835 for the discussion of public questions such as statehood for Michigan, capital punishment, slavery, and temperance. The Ladies' Library Association, organized in the 1840s, was the first such group in

the state and the third in the nation. This group sponsored public lectures and accumulated a circulating library of books, sculptures, paintings, and natural history displays years before the opening of the first public library and museum in the state.

With this kind of intellectual environment, the county provided a receptive audience for visiting speakers, including Frederick Douglass and Horace Greeley. Mark Twain visited Kalamazoo to speak on *Roughing It.* Ralph Waldo Emerson lectured "On Manners," and dropped in on a class at Kalamazoo College that was discussing his philosophy.

Like today, early residents of Kalamazoo County possessed a lively interest in music. In addition to supporting local groups such as the Philharmonic Society, the German Lyric Society, and the Mozart Mannechor, residents welcomed performances by the Boston Philharmonic Club, the Mendelssohn Quintette, and the Jubilee Singers during the 1870s. A state musical convention was held in Kalamazoo in 1855.

A visitor commented on the quality of life enjoyed in Kalamazoo County during the past century:

I often wonder where the poor people live, for I have seen none but comfortable and few but pretty residences, and there are no people from whom a supply of domestic service can be drawn; the consequence is that many, even wealthy, ladies keep no servants, but do their own work, and prepare all the meals of the family in the nicest and cosiest of kitchens, many of which are really elegant in their appoint-

Parsons Business College, established in 1869, helped put Kalamazoo on the map via talented alumni like W.K. Kellogg of cereal fame, and Calvin Forbes, whose "Kalamazoo Croquet" sets were the rage throughout the nation. Courtesy, The Michigan Stock Shop

The Ladies' Library Association, organized in the 1840s, was the first such group in the state and third in the nation. Courtesy, The Michigan Stock Shop

Right: One of the earliest successes of the area's fertile farmlands was the crop that gave Kalamazoo the whimsical nickname of Celery City. Courtesy, The Michigan Stock Shop

ments. How they can do this and yet find time not only to visit and receive company, but also to read and prepare papers on history, science, and art, to be read at their club, is mysterious to me.

Without a doubt this fashionable visitor had an overly idealized view of Kalamazoo, but visitors today often entertain a similar stereotype. There is poverty and turmoil in Kalamazoo, but perhaps less than in other urban areas of comparable size. Even during Michigan's auto industry "depression" in the 1970s, Kalamazoo County's diversified industrial base kept its employment rate stable. Perhaps equally important, the leading families of the community have established a strong tradition of private philanthropy, providing funds not only to support the arts and education but also to provide an effective network of human services.

If fault can be found with Kalamazoo, it is that residents go about their business as if they were living in a much smaller community—and in a much less complicated era. With a fully developed industrial base and the cultural and educational advantages of a major metropolitan area, Kalamazoo in many ways retains the qualities that attracted the early settlers and native peoples before them. It is a good place to live and make a living.

Centers of Commerce

The James River Corporation specializes in state-of-the-art manufacturing of a variety of fine packaging products. Photo by John Gilroy/The Michigan Stock Shop

Early villages grew quickly in Kalamazoo County and met basic needs. They typically included a gristmill to process the harvest of the land, a sawmill to provide lumber and building supplies, a general store, and a hotel.

Schoolcraft was the first, and for many years the most populous, of these commercial centers. Every Saturday, settlers from near and far gathered at the Big Island Hotel. *The History of Kalamazoo County* reports that the hotel was "a point of rendezvous for the 'characters' of the new settlement . . . It was a place of much business, and over its bar were dispensed the various liquid decoctions common to the day and place, while horse races, fights, and other amusements were progressing outside." In a frame structure to the east of the Big Island was Smith, Huston & Co., the first general store in the area. Less adventurous and more practical settlers gathered there from scattered points throughout the area: Three Rivers, Paw Paw, Otsego, Allegan, Battle Creek, and even Marshall.

Horace H. Comstock was determined to have the town named after him designated as the county seat, and he saw to it that Comstock village became a thriving commercial center. In Galesburg, which was also competing to be the county seat, Philip Gray built the first store as well as the first tavern. When he brought in a wagon load of goods for sale, he would put a sign in front of his store with the words: "This store will be closed for three days to enable the proprietor to mark and arrange his very large stock of new goods!"

In the end, Titus Bronson succeeded in having the village he founded selected as the county seat. In 1834 the federal land office was moved there from White Pigeon, bringing throngs of settlers eager to buy land to the community. From then on the village of Bronson—now the city of Kalamazoo—was clearly destined to become the commercial center of the county.

From the Kalamazoo House to the Kalamazoo Center

In his original plat of the village, Titus Bronson apparently intended Kalamazoo Avenue to serve as the city's center; it was a broad thoroughfare and was well situated. But when General Justus Burdick—one of the major investors in Titus Bronson's town—erected the Kalamazoo House hotel, he chose to locate on what is now Michigan Avenue, near where Portage angles off to the south. It became, and continues to be, the unofficial center of the Kalamazoo business district.

Schoolcraft merchant H.B. Huston soon opened a store nearby, and by 1836 the village had four hotels, a printing office, four tailors, a silversmith, a furniture store, a dry goods establishment, a jewelry store, a drugstore, a bootery, a bank, and the area's first newspaper. When the population reached 5,000 by 1854, Kalamazoo had 150 stores, 2 banking houses, and 2 weekly newspapers.

Kalamazoo's commercial district expanded along South Burdick Street during the 1880s, led primarily by a pair of enterprising brothers from Belfast, Ireland. John Gilmore moved to Kalamazoo in 1881, married a local woman, and opened a dry goods store in a 25-foot storefront. His rent was relatively cheap—only $20.83 a month. Two years later James Gilmore joined his brother, and they soon moved to larger quarters on the east side of the street. By the turn of the century the store was selling more than $150,000 worth of merchandise a year.

By 1910 the Gilmore brothers had passed away, but James' widow, Carrie, incorporated the firm as Gilmore Brothers. She secured a loan and enlarged the store to the six-story structure that has been a landmark in downtown Kalamazoo for more than 100 years.

As early as 1925 Gilmore Brothers recognized the importance of downtown parking. Buying the old Farmers' Sheds property, they provided ample parking right behind the store. A multi-level parking garage, with a ramp to the store, now occupies that area. In October 1987 Gilmore Brothers announced plans for a major renovation of its downtown building to convert parts of the building to office space.

The Nation's First Downtown Mall

During the 1950s, faced with growing competition from shopping centers on the outskirts of the city, downtown merchants and property owners moved to revitalize the central business district. A major redevelopment effort was launched with the formation of the Downtown Kalamazoo Association. It resulted in the nation's first downtown mall, opened on August 19, 1959, to the music of Tommy Dorsey's band. Two blocks of Burdick Street were transformed into a permanent pedestrian mall with trees, fountains, park benches, and a playground. Another two blocks were added later.

As a complement to the mall, the city joined with Inland Steel Development Corporation in 1972 to finance and build the Kalamazoo Center. Located near the site of General Burdick's original Kalamazoo House, this 10-level Hilton hotel and convention center includes retail shops, offices, restaurants, a cinema, and a health club. With these up-to-date facilities and an aggressive campaign by the Convention and Visitor's Bureau of the Kalamazoo County Chamber of Commerce, the size of the city's previously

dormant convention industry was more than tripled.

In recent years developers have taken advantage of the continuing interest in downtown Kalamazoo. The historic Haymarket Building on Michigan Avenue was completely renovated to provide office space and elegant quarters for Oakley's Restau-

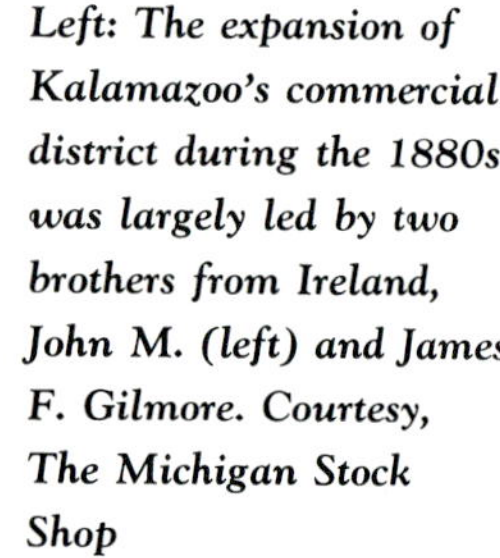

Left: The expansion of Kalamazoo's commercial district during the 1880s was largely led by two brothers from Ireland, John M. (left) and James F. Gilmore. Courtesy, The Michigan Stock Shop

Above left: This prosperous-looking building was the second incarnation of the Gilmore Brothers business, which started in a 25-foot storefront across the street in the early 1880s. Courtesy, The Michigan Stock Shop

Above: One of the first hotels in the area, Kalamazoo House was located at the head of Portage Street on what is now East Michigan Avenue. Courtesy, The Michigan Stock Shop

Above right: The historic Haymarket Building on Michigan Avenue is one example of Kalamazoo's enthusiasm for integrating its heritage with modern development. Photo by John Gilroy/The Michigan Stock Shop

rant on the ground floor. Nearby businesses and the Biggs/Gilmore advertising agency have renovated their buildings to preserve and emphasize historical architecture. On the south side of the mall, the Hinman Company's Skyrise Center and Century Plaza developments provide modernistic office and apartment space. The Cornerstone Building at Park and West Michigan has revitalized the west side of the downtown area.

To provide a plan for the continuing redevelopment and revitalization of the central business district, in December 1988 the Kalamazoo City Commission approved "The Downtown Tomorrow Agenda for Progress." This plan sets up a creative financing strategy to fund major public improvements without burdening homeowners in the city, plus a process for seeking consensus on a redevelopment program that meets the needs of existing businesses, potential developers, and users of the downtown. Through tax incre-

ment financing, taxes deriving from new growth in the downtown area will be used to fund public improvements in the area that will in turn attract additional development. Downtown Kalamazoo, Inc. (DKI) was created as the one group responsible for overseeing redevelopment efforts and for managing the delivery of key services such as parking and mall maintenance. The ultimate goal is to have a central business district that serves as an appropriate centerpiece for the community—reflecting the city's past as well as representing its aspirations for the future.

Portage: Shopping Centers and Planned Living Units

Always a thriving rural community, Portage became an important commercial center during the 1940s when The Upjohn Company built its major manufacturing complex on Portage Road. While most Upjohn research is carried out at its new complex in downtown Kalamazoo, the company's manufacturing facilities and international headquarters are situated on more than 1,500 acres of what was once Michigan farmland. With ample space for parking, recreational facilities, and future expansion, the Upjohn property is close to Portage and Kalamazoo, yet comfortably isolated from residential and shopping areas. The Kalamazoo County Airport is nearby, only a few miles north on Portage Road.

The commercial centers of Portage have congregated on a busy commercial strip along South Westnedge Avenue. Major complexes are clustered around Meijer Thrifty Acres, near the Kalamazoo/Portage boundary; Southland Mall, just south of Interstate 94 highway; and Crossroads Mall, farther south near the corner of Romence Road.

A Gilmore Brothers branch has served as an anchor for the Southland Mall for many years. Faced by increased competition from other shopping centers, Southland Mall redefined its market niche several years ago—primarily through the addition of a highly successful specialty retailer, T.J. Maxx, and other stores designed to appeal to value-conscious families and career-oriented women.

Crossroads Mall, opened in 1980, is the county's largest shopping center and the first multilevel shopping complex in out-state Michigan. It includes outlets of Hudson's, J.C. Penney, Mervyn's, and Sears along with more than 100 other businesses.

In addition to these centers, numerous mini-malls located along South Westnedge, Portage Street, Oakland Drive, and Romence have expanded the shopping alternatives.

Now the second-largest municipality in the county, with 40,000 residents, Portage offers comfortable living in suburban subdivisions or in condominium and apartment complexes. Many are targeted at young professionals. An example of the planned living complexes becoming increasingly common in Portage is The Moors. The attractive complex, set on 600 rolling, tree-lined acres, includes an 18-hole golf course, tennis courts, a health club, swimming pools, and several retail and office centers. Residents have the advantages of living in a wooded, natural environment with open-space buffers, while at the same time having access to a full range of community and social amenities.

Oshtemo: Balanced Development

For those living to the west of Kalamazoo in Kalamazoo Township and for the growing number who have chosen to build in

the semirural areas of Oshtemo Township, Westmain and Maple Hill malls provide comprehensive shopping services along the West Main Street commercial strip.

Montgomery Ward, Gilmore Brothers, and Steketee's are longtime residents of Maple Hill. The mall was extended to the west in the early 1980s through an expansion of Meijer Thrifty Acres market into a Meijer Square Discount Center.

Westmain Mall, the oldest enclosed shopping complex in the area, has suffered vacancies since the departure of a large J.C. Penney store. The discount retailer Zayre continues to do a healthy business at one end

The interior court of the Kalamazoo Center attracts throngs of residents and out-of-towners to its restaurants, movies, and other businesses. The multiuse complex is at Michigan Avenue and Park Street. Photo by John A. Lacko/The Michigan Stock Shop

Shoppers can visit Cross-roads Mall well into the evening hours. Photo by John A. Lacko/The Michigan Stock Shop

of the mall and Jewel-Osco, a grocery/drug chain, recently took over a good part of the space vacated by J.C. Penney—a move which should attract other tenants.

Rural areas of Oshtemo are at present among the most popular parts of the county for residential and commercial developments.

Comstock: Now an Industrial Center

The days when Comstock was a bustling frontier community with a general store, a tavern, the Baldwin House hotel, four gristmills, and a sawmill are long past. Even the small number of local shops that have survived are gradually being replaced by increased competition from the East Towne shopping complex at the corner of Gull Road and Sprinkle. Major stores here include K mart and Meijer Thrifty Acres.

Over the past 25 years Comstock has evolved into a busy industrial center. With the opening of the General Motors stamping plant in October 1965, Comstock began to attract a number of industrial employers: Bemis and Son, Inc., makers of highway signs and barricading material; Newhouse Printers' Supply; Aero-Motive, Inc.,

makers of industrial reels and related items; Wheeler-Blaney Co., mechanical contractors; and Total Plastics, Inc. These companies provide employment for those living throughout the greater Kalamazoo metropolitan area.

Comstock provides suburban living for persons employed throughout the county. Ambitious new apartment complexes are being planned in the Gull Road area.

Comstock, with a population of 11,300, was one of the first townships in the county to have its own library and fire department, an elected park board, and an extensive park system. In 1984 a bond issue allowed Comstock to expand its library and its township office complex.

Richland: Upscale Living

Many years ago Richland was a prominent farm community, with a grain elevator and a railroad that serviced it. Today it is a well-maintained community that offers attractive suburban, lakeside, and semirural living. Many of the county's prominent professionals and business leaders live in the Richland area and around nearby Gull Lake.

Most downtown businesses have been

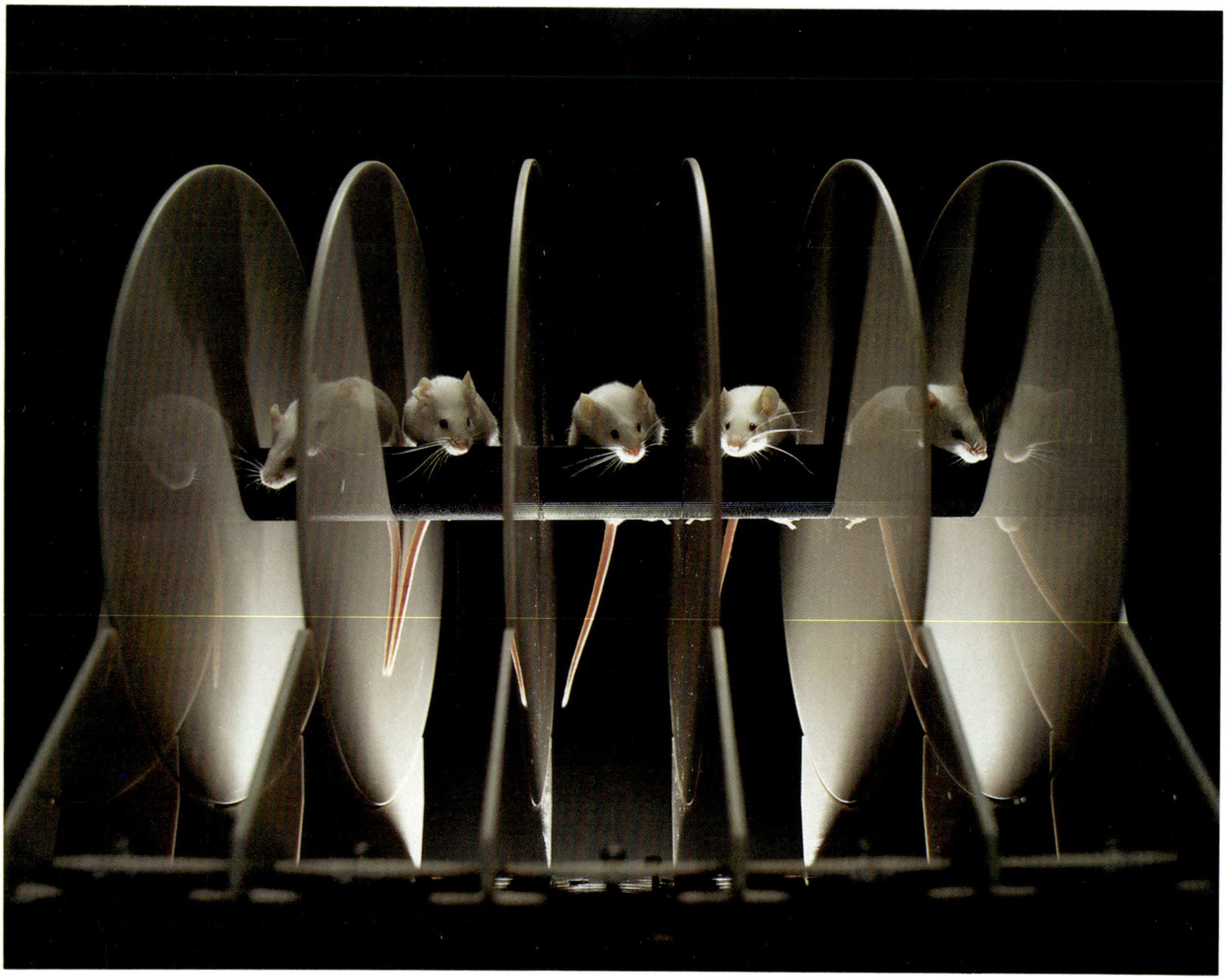

Above: Most of The Up-john Company's research is carried out at its new complex in downtown Kalamazoo. Photo by John Gilroy/The Michigan Stock Shop

Left: The arrival of The Upjohn Company in the 1940s was a major turning point in the development of Portage as a commercial center. Photo by John Gilroy/The Michigan Stock Shop

Above and below: In a town called Parchment, the James River Corporation stepped into historic shoes when it moved onto the well-kept grounds of the old Kalamazoo Vegetable Parchment Company. KVP had been more an institution than just a company, its owner Jacob Kindleberger taking a paternalistic interest in the morals and life-styles of his employees. KVP's modern successor is more inclined to mind its own business, which is state-of-the-art manufacturing of a variety of fine packaging products. Photo by John Gilroy/The Michigan Stock Shop

rebuilt or revamped over the past 15 to 20 years, and the shops in Richland reflect the diversity of the surrounding community: three financial institutions (more than the norm for a town of 700); Weber's Village Market, with a reputation for some of the finest cuts of meats in the area; Serafino's Party Store, where one can pick up a bottle or two of Mouton Rothschild or a case of Pepsi-Cola; and the neat and well-stocked Richland Lumber Yard and Home Center. In a mini-mall on the outskirts of town, The Cab-

inetry offers a range of gift items plus distinctive furniture—purchased off of floor displays or handmade to the customer's specifications.

The picturesque Gull Lake area witnesses some influx of summer visitors from Chicago, Detroit, and other Midwestern cities, but the majority of homes now are occupied year-round. Merchants agree that the business climate is stable. When Jack Weber's Village Market building, a landmark of the square since 1897, burned down some years ago, 11 of his regular customers banded together to ensure he had financial backing to rebuild.

The Upjohn Company's Asgrow agricultural chemical facility is located on the highway halfway between Comstock and Richland. Other major employers in the Richland area include Richard-Allan Medical Industries (laboratory, surgical, and operating room supplies), Parker Hannifin Corporation's pneumatic division (filters, regulators, lubricators, air valves), several marinas, Beardsley & Co. (advertising agency), and Village Graphics (lithographic plates and processing).

Vicksburg: Paper City

Vicksburg owes its name to John Vickers, who in 1831 built a gristmill on spring-fed Portage Creek. In the twentieth century, how-

ever,
tity
son
time
firm
Lee
burg
wate
ing

pany
than
Abo
diat
Sim
burg
cent
$5-
its

mo
and

Pa
Eve
its
tov
bar
idl
me
pap
foo
wi
to

str
an
th
m
th
"U
cle
th
pl
va
E
ta

ri
p
P
R
ti
t
c
v

The Episcopal Diocese of Western Michigan has its headquarters in Kala-mazoo; its Cathedral Church of Christ the King is a local landmark. Photo by John D. Strauss

P at Schafer's grandparents once owned a square block of land near Lake Shore Drive in Chicago. They moved to Kalamazoo early this century because they felt it "was a good place to raise children."

Moses Walker's parents moved to Kalamazoo from Mississippi in the late 1930s, during the Great Depression. "Times were hard, and my dad came to take a job at the National Gypsum paper mill," Walker said.

Schafer is now co-owner of Schafer's Flowers, a landmark in Westwood Plaza since 1955. In 1987 Schafer and her brother opened a second shop in the upscale Woodbridge Hills shopping center in Portage. Walker is president of DeLano Clinic, the mental health arm of Borgess Medical Center. Both have lived virtually their entire lives in Kalamazoo.

"Kalamazoo County is a good place to do business," Schafer said. "The population has grown tremendously over the period I can remember, but the people have always been very friendly and open. You can have good rapport with customers you've come to know over many years."

Walker's view is similar. "I've always liked Kalamazoo—felt it was a good and decent place to live," he said. "It's small enough and friendly enough that you can have a personal interaction with all kinds of people. Yet those who come in from the outside are always shocked at the level of sophistication."

A community leader who has served terms on the Kalamazoo City Commission and the Kalamazoo Board of Education, Walker likes to tell a story about his friend who visited from Washington, D.C.:

I was executive director of the Douglass Community Association at that time, and I took him along to one of our Saturday morning meetings. At the meeting was the city manager, the superintendent of schools, the county prosecutor, and several members of the city commission. He was shocked. Where in the world could you go to a meeting and have access to that assemblage of people? Certainly not in Washington, D.C.

For Moses Walker, Pat Schafer, and others, Kalamazoo County offers something that other places cannot match—a quality of life that is impossible to reduce to a numerical ranking.

Newcomers to the county soon recognize this quality, and so do those who return after moving away. "I simply had forgotten how easy life can be here," said a woman who had moved from Kalamazoo County to take a university teaching job in Massachusetts, then returned for an extended visit with friends. "I had to go downtown in the middle of the day. Within minutes I had a parking space in the garage at the Kalamazoo Center. I was used to paying at least five dollars for downtown parking, but in Kalamazoo, the charge was less than a dollar!" Within half an hour, this woman had completed her business and was back home.

Despite grumbles about the rush hour traffic on South Westnedge Avenue between Kalamazoo and Portage, residents of Kalamazoo do not have to tie up hours of their life in traffic snarls, searching frantically for parking spaces. From his home on the north side of Kalamazoo, Moses Walker can be at his office in 5 to 10 minutes— "in heavy traffic, when I'm not in a hurry!" From her apartment in a historic home near downtown Kalamazoo, Pat Schafer can get to her shop in Woodbridge Hills—on the far outskirts of Portage—in 10 to 15 minutes.

Probably no one in the county lives more than 15 minutes away from a lake, or more than 40 minutes from a Lake Michigan beach. For those who like the excitement of city life, Chicago and Detroit are only two and a half hours away by interstate highway or rail—close enough for a day trip, yet far enough to justify a holiday weekend for shopping, baseball, and dining. The Kalamazoo County Airport offers convenient service to most major cities in the country.

A playground at a downtown mall makes a shopping trip into a family affair. This little haven is typical of a city known as a good place to raise children. Photo by John Gilroy/The Michigan Stock Shop

And while Kalamazoo is hardly the Sunbelt, the area offers moderate summers, colorful autumns, and winter conditions that are ideal for cross-country and downhill skiing—abundant snow with temperatures moderated somewhat by Lake Michigan.

Growth Without Growing Pains

Kalamazoo County has experienced gradual, steady growth in population and economic development, without growing pains or rough edges. When Pat Schafer's father opened his Westwood Plaza store in 1955, there was nothing else in the area except cornfields. "You could pull out onto West Main without even looking!" Schafer said with a laugh. Today Westwood Plaza is a thriving crossroads of commercial activity, while Schafer's shop in Woodbridge Hills is surrounded by woods and farmland—and a burgeoning population neatly tucked away in condominiums and planned living developments.

The paper industry that brought Moses Walker's father to town continues to provide jobs in the area. As it has matured, the paper industry has been supplemented by a healthy, diverse economic base. Kalamazoo's manufacturing sector consistently outperforms the rest of the state and the nation in employment growth.

According to *Business Outlook* (a publication of the W.E. Upjohn Institute for Employ-

ment Research), employment in paper products, transportation, and food products followed the national trend during 1987. At the same time drugs, fabricated metals, miscellaneous durable goods, and other industries found Kalamazoo to be a particularly advantageous location, growing here at a rate much higher than the national averages for those industries. The unemployment rate for the county in January 1989 was 5.0 percent—compared to 7.8 percent for the state as a whole.

The largest employer in the county, with 8,400 employees, is The Upjohn Company—followed by General Motors with 3,300. Next, with more than 2,000 employees each, come three public institutions: Western Michigan University, Bronson Methodist Hospital, and Borgess Medical Center. Others in the top 10 are James River Corp. (paper products), the Kalamazoo Public Schools, NWL Control Systems (military guidance systems), Meijer, Inc. (groceries and household products), and the Stryker Corp. (medical supplies).

With education and health care accounting for more than 20,000 jobs in a labor force of 113,500, the county has an unusually large percentage of trained professionals who expect, and find, excellent cultural and educational resources. Pat Schafer attended Catholic schools in the Texas Corners/ Mattawan area, where she lived as a child,

Below: Convenient service to most of the country's major cities starts at the up-to-date Kalamazoo County Airport. Photo by Patricia A. Bulthuis

and in Kalamazoo. Moses Walker, one of nine children in his family, went to Lincoln Elementary on the north side and old Kalamazoo Central High before earning his bachelor's degree from Western Michigan University. "I believe in public education, and I feel comfortable sending my kids to public schools in Kalamazoo," Walker said. "I certainly wouldn't if I lived in Detroit or Chicago."

Walker earned a master's degree in social work from Wayne State University while serving as administrative assistant to Detroit mayor Coleman Young, and is working to obtain a master's of business administra-

tion from Western Michigan University. Four of his brothers and sisters are college graduates; three have advanced degrees.

"I can understand that young black professionals might be critical of Kalamazoo from the social point of view. By virtue of numbers alone, you simply don't have the range and variety of social opportunities you might find in a big city," Walker said. He pointed out, however, that the situation is changing with the influx of black professionals during the past several years.

"In terms of race, you see pretty much the same situation here as you do anywhere else," Walker said. "Blacks suffer unemployment and underemployment at a much greater rate than the general population. And most blacks live in older, deteriorating housing in the inner city. A lot of problems still exist, but Kalamazoo is a progressive community in terms of *concern* about race relations." Walker pointed out that a number of black citizens, including Judge Charles Pratt, the late educator Pauline Johnson, and former Kalamazoo city manager Robert Bobb, have "demonstrated to all that a black can contribute as much as anyone else if given the opportunity to provide community leadership."

According to the 1980 census, blacks made up 7.5 percent of the county's population, living mostly in the city, Kalamazoo Township, and Oshtemo. The black population in the city was 15.6 percent in 1980 and is expected to approach 20 percent by 1990. With more black professionals coming to the area, these housing patterns might change. In the meantime, both black and white leaders in the community have demonstrated a commitment to restore and maintain inner-city neighborhoods.

Good Housing at Low Prices

Real estate throughout the county is characterized by its diversity and—by East and West Coast standards—low prices. Now designated as historical areas, the South Street and Stuart Street areas near downtown Kalamazoo offer Victorian residences, some restored as single-family homes and others converted to elegant apartments or bed-and-breakfast establishments. Many well-maintained houses built during the first three decades of the twentieth century can be found along Bronson Boulevard, on Westnedge Hill, and in smaller communities

Above left: In terms of location, cost of living, cultural opportunities, and more, Kalamazoo is a uniquely livable environment. Photo by John Gilroy/The Michigan Stock Shop

Left: The pharmaceutical industry is just one of several that have enjoyed faster growth in Kalamazoo than in the rest of the nation; The Upjohn Company is the prime example. Photo by John Gilroy/The Michigan Stock Shop

such as Richland, Schoolcraft, and Augusta. Three- or four-bedroom homes in these areas generally sell in the $40,000 to $70,000 range.

Newer homes are available in the Winchell and Milwood neighborhoods and throughout the suburban areas of Portage and Oshtemo. Those desiring elegant lakeside living can find it on Gull Lake, near Richland, and on Indian Lake, near Vicksburg. New housing and planned-living complexes are being initiated almost daily in semirural areas near Portage, Oshtemo, and Comstock.

According to figures released by the Kalamazoo Board of Realtors, the average selling price of a home in the area during 1987 was $56,355, with most homes selling in the $30,000 to $60,000 range. That year witnessed a 36 percent increase in the number of houses selling for $120,000 or more, and a 25 percent decline in the number of homes selling in the $100,000 to $120,000 range.

In December 1987 *Home*, a buyer's catalog published by the Kalamazoo Board of Realtors, listed the following description of what a buyer could expect to purchase for $125,000:

AN INDOOR HEATED POOL is hidden behind this fine family home with four large bedrooms, family room with loft, third bath in finished basement. Over 3,000 square feet with 10 rooms. Situated on a double lot with an extra garage on Edgemoor just south of Kleinstuck Preserve. Asking $125,000 with low cost seller financing available.

Property taxes in Kalamazoo County are levied against the state equalized value (SEV) of a property, which is figured at 50 percent of the market value. For a home selling for $50,000 (an SEV of $25,000), 1986 taxes ranged from $1,042 in Vicksburg to $1,762 in Kalamazoo.

More than 70 percent of property taxes in the county are used to pay for public education. The rest go toward city, county, and township operating expenses and special assessments to finance road, water, and sewer projects. Even though property taxes have risen consistently, increases in the past few years have been moderate.

Access to Housing: A Community Issue

Several organizations to help rebuild decaying neighborhoods and provide housing for those with low and moderate income levels have sprung up in Kalamazoo, through the combined support of churches and human service agencies with voluntary initiative and labor. The most visible include the Northside Nonprofit Housing Corporation, the Northside Association for Community Development, Center City Housing, Inc., and the Kalamazoo Valley Habitat for Humanity.

To aid the efforts of these local groups while allowing them to maintain their autonomy, The Upjohn Company in July 1987 made a large donation as a challenge grant to the Local Initiative Support Corporation (LISC), a national organization that helps administer and fund projects undertaken by voluntary groups. A local LISC group was then set up to seek donations from other area corporations and use the money to help viable groups already working in the com-

munity.

Within months, the Kalamazoo LISC was able to help fund a project of the Kalamazoo Valley Habitat for Humanity. After purchasing for one dollar three houses on Upjohn land originally targeted for demolition, Habitat moved them to three vacant lots in Portage—a project that was completed with a great deal of volunteer effort and cooperation. Habitat then renovated the houses—as they have many other proper-

Left: When the bright lights beckon, Kalamazoo residents can head for the big city via convenient rail service. Both Chicago and Detroit are only two and one-half hours away. Photo by Patricia A. Bulthuis

Right: Kalamazoo's tremendous variety of architecture includes many Victorian and early twentieth-century homes in excellent condition. Some have been converted to other uses, but many are available—and surprisingly affordable—as family homes. Photo by Patricia A. Bulthuis

Above: This is an aerial view of the community of South Westnedge. Photo by John Gilroy/ The Michigan Stock Shop

Left: The 1980 census indicates blacks comprise 7.5 percent of the county's population. Photo by Patricia A. Bulthuis

ties in the area—for sale to low and moderate income families.

Committed to providing access to good housing, Habitat for Humanity has had remarkable success in mobilizing and coordinating volunteer efforts from all sectors of the community. Habitat operations manager Steve Senesi works closely with local builders and suppliers, getting labor and materials donated or offered at cost. During 1988 the Home Builders Association of Kalamazoo joined Habitat in a project to build two new houses on vacant lots in Kalamazoo by donating labor, materials, and cash.

This blend of corporate and private philanthropy has become recognized, over many years, as a unique element of the quality of life in Kalamazoo County. Helen Coover, who has worked for more than 50 years building a network of services for seniors in the community, recalled the challenge gift during the 1950s that resulted in the founding of Senior Services, Inc. A former public school teacher, Coover was a pioneer in starting community programs for the elderly—but she had reached a bureaucratic dead end in her efforts to start a program through the Kalamazoo Recreation Department. As Coover told the story:

I was on my way to the post office one day when I ran into a prominent member of the community. He said he'd heard about the things I'd been trying to do and asked how much I needed to get a good program started. I told him I'd need $5,000 a year, and he pulled out his checkbook right there.

Later channeled through the United Way, that $5,000 yearly donation was the start of a one-woman Committee on Aging that grew into a score of volunteer programs. "I didn't have a car," Coover said, "but a nickel bus ride would take me anywhere in the city. I got around, and I had a ball. Most social service agencies offer programs we think people need, but I wanted to talk to people and find out what kind of programs *they* thought they needed."

Going to the United Women's Church Council for help, Coover formed a core of volunteers who provided rides for seniors—to do their shopping, go to the doctor, or merely visit friends. Through one program, elderly citizens made mittens for children and lap robes for seniors in nursing homes. The gardening project involved seniors in planting, harvesting, and delivering fresh vegetables for those who needed them. The clothing project gathered and recycled used clothing. The "Friendly Visitors' Club" paid regular social calls to several hundred lonely seniors.

Now 77 and officially retired, Helen Coover continues her "friendly" visits and her vegetable and clothing projects. Working 40 to 45 hours a week (reduced from the 80 to 85 hours she used to work when she earned a paycheck), she is a member of the State Commission on Aging, the State Gerontology Society, and the Helen Coover Emergency Fund. Her pioneering spirit and energy have given birth to a well-organized and efficient network of senior services: Care-a-Van, Meals on Wheels, and the Helen Coover Social and Recreation Center (operated by the city until 1988). A number of apartment complexes, specifically designed to meet the social and physical needs of seniors, have been constructed with the help of federal and state grants and loans.

Meeting Human Needs

More than 300 human service agencies in Kalamazoo County meet the needs of all age groups, providing counseling, aftercare,

Right: The area's many beautiful parks are another reason why so many families with children locate in Kalamazoo. Photo by John Gilroy/The Michigan Stock Shop

Facing page top: While Kalamazoo is not necessarily a "church town" religious values have and will continue to play a significant role in the community. Photo by John Gilroy/The Michigan Stock Shop

Right: Many thriving farms are located near Kalamazoo, shipping fresh produce to its communities every day. Photo by John Gilroy/The Michigan Stock Shop

Facing page below left: The Cathedral Church of Christ the King, an Episcopal church, is a dramatic feature of the local landscape. Photo by John Gilroy/The Michigan Stock Shop

Facing page below right: Churchgoers take time to visit outside the Friendship Missionary Baptist Church. Photo by John D. Strauss

Universalist Peoples Church has a particularly strong tradition, having brought Caroline Bartlett Crane to town as pastor in 1889. A feminist of national renown, Crane started a number of innovative programs that were later incorporated into public school curriculums—including kindergarten, gym for girls, manual training, and domestic science.

Socially concerned individuals need only stop by the Kalamazoo Deacons' Conference (of the Christian Reformed Church) on the north side or the Eighth Day Bookstore operated by the Reverend Gerald Diment and the Shalom Community on South Westnedge to get a quick rundown on current issues, unmet needs, and ongoing projects.

A casual visitor to Kalamazoo, noticing the stately old churches that line Bronson Park, might assume that Kalamazoo is "a church town." This is not necessarily true even though religious values have played and will continue to play a significant role in the community. Rather, the circle of churches in the center of town is a sign that the people who came to this area many years ago liked what they found. They decided that Kalamazoo County is a good place to lay a foundation.

The Cultural Tradition

Kalamazoo is a colorful city, with much to enjoy in the areas of art and entertainment. This fireworks display took place in front of the First Reformed Church (left) and the county courthouse. Photo by John A. Lacko/ The Michigan Stock Shop

C ulture plays a leading role in Kalamazoo. Those who live here want to stay, and those who move here want to come—largely due to the abundant cultural opportunities. In terms of both quality and diversity, they feel that Kalamazoo County rivals Grand Rapids and Ann Arbor as a center for culture and the arts.

A capsule history of the arts in Kalamazoo County is embedded in a two-block area of downtown Kalamazoo consisting of the Ladies' Library Building, built in 1879 in the style of a gracious home; the Civic Auditorium, with its spacious lobby and crystal chandeliers reflecting the sophistication of the 1920s; the Art Center, functional and modern in design; and the Carver Center, built in 1958 to provide additional space for the Kalamazoo Symphony as well as the Civic Players. Other facilities spread through the area meet the needs of a culture-oriented population, the most visible being the Dalton Center Recital Hall at Western Michigan University, the Wellspring Dance Collaborative in the old Saniwax Building, the New Vic Theater in a residential neighborhood near downtown Kalamazoo, the Light Fine Arts Building at Kalamazoo College, and the Barn Theater in Augusta. About 70 nonprofit organizations, covering all of the performing and visual arts, function actively in the county.

In 1985 the Arts Council of Greater Kalamazoo conducted a survey to document the impact of the arts on Kalamazoo County, and the results were impressive. Of a population of 218,000, more than 118,000 persons are or have enrolled in arts-related educational programs—not including those taking formal classes through the schools or universities. In 1985 more than 1,000 arts events were held, drawing a combined audience of 875,000.

In 1985 the arts created 500 full- and part-time jobs (in addition to more than 100,000 volunteer hours), accounted for $10 million in direct and indirect spending, and paid $265,000 in income and other taxes. For every dollar invested in a nonprofit arts organization, the county reaped a return of $7.70. "We've always talked about the contribution the arts make toward our quality of life," said Gayle Hoogstraten, executive director of the Arts Council. "However, the survey shows us that the arts also make a significant contribution to our economy. If you took away the arts, we simply would not be as well off."

The arts flourish today primarily because of a rich tradition started in the nineteenth century by groups such as the Ladies' Library Association and the Kalamazoo Lyceum. Long before the community had a public library or museum, the Ladies' Library Association organized several thousands of books for general circulation and exhibited sculptures, paintings, and natural history displays. Together with the Lyceum, they sponsored an array of stimulating lectures, readings, musicals, and stage presentations, serving as a "school of culture" for the community.

In its Kalamazoo Centennial edition on January 24, 1937, the *Kalamazoo Gazette* credited Albert May Todd, founder of the A.M. Todd Company, with contributing to the development of a "definite city wide interest in art." To quote the *Gazette*:

Roaming with knap-sack and staff, he (Todd) had begun travels in Europe in 1875, and had visited the noted art galleries of the Continent. This led him to assemble one of the largest collections of paintings (both originals and copies), archeological objects, and rare books at that time in the mid-west. Through loan exhibits at the colleges, schools and other public institutions, his collections were made available to the public and served to center an interest in art.

Private Gifts for Public Benefit

In the twentieth century, wealthy individuals and families played a major role in providing facilities for the arts. Ann Louise Raymond, a local woman from a German immigrant family, married a

Chicago hardware wholesaler, but her heart remained in Kalamazoo. She returned often—by taxicab—to write checks to local arts organizations. With the cab waiting, she would visit her bank (she continued to do her banking in Kalamazoo), then jump back in the cab for the 140-mile return trip. Her donations of money and works of art formed the original endowment that helped carry the Kalamazoo Institute of Arts through its first three decades. Ralph Harmon Booth, a member of the family that founded Booth Newspapers, donated additional money during the 1930s for art scholarships and, later, a work of art. (The *Kalamazoo Gazette* is a Booth newspaper.)

The Civic Auditorium was built in 1921 and donated to "the people of Kalamazoo" by William E. Upjohn. His daughter, Dorothy Upjohn Dalton, was a loyal follower of the Kalamazoo Civic Players—attending productions, acting in many, and later providing her own financial support. Donald and Genevieve Gilmore donated money for the construction of the million-dollar Art Center building, dedicated in 1961.

The late Irving Gilmore's generosity to local musicians has provided the basis for a number of local legends. For example, when composer Curtis Curtis-Smith was seeking financing to help purchase a very special nineteenth-century grand piano, Gilmore's response was one that others in the community had heard many times before: "Well, how much money does he need? Would he accept a gift?"

"These families had a sincere appreciation of the arts, and it was not elitist," said Gayle Hoogstraten. "They wanted the arts to be accessible to people in the community, and they provided the facilities to make that possible."

In recent years this personal giving has become institutionalized and is now channeled mainly through foundations: the Kalamazoo Foundation, the Harold and Grace Upjohn Foundation, the Irving Gilmore Foundation, and the Dorothy Dalton Foundation. Corporations have realized that a gift to the arts in Kalamazoo is not charity but an investment. The Upjohn Company gave $75,400 to support local arts during 1986.

When major gifts are made for a building or endowment—particularly through the Kalamazoo Foundation—the procedure is the same. A board of trustees is set up to over-

see and assume responsibility for the donation. The organization's elected board of directors continues as a separate entity, answering to the membership and assuming responsibility for programs and operating expenses. This dual-board arrangement is designed to provide both stability and flexibility, and it works well. Financial support, often sorely needed during the early years of the community and even through the 1930s, is now forthcoming . . . but never at the expense of the individual effort that has been crucial to the development of the arts in Kalamazoo County.

A project undertaken in 1987 to erect a memorial to Dr. Martin Luther King, Jr., at a recently renovated and renamed park on the north side, demonstrates the county's high regard for art. With a grant from the Irving Gilmore Foundation and a large gift from a private donor, the Kalamazoo County Public Art Commission mobilized an effort to find a suitable piece of public sculpture. A jury of nationally recognized artists and critics was asked to choose the finalists out of 109 applications received from across the country and the community made the final selection—a work by Lisa Reinertson of Chico, California. The sculpture is a portrait of King in stride. Inset in his religious robe are scenes from black history; on his shoulders are the two persons who influenced him the most: his wife, Coretta, and Mahatma Gandhi.

"This was a perfect example of the way the community works together," said Hoogstraten. "We already had an active Public Art Commission, so when the opportunity

Above: Banners outside of the Kalamazoo Civic Auditorium announce its varied theatrical offerings. Built in 1921, the interior sports the lavish, crystal-chandeliered interior design typical of the period. Photo by Charlene Farris

Top right: This statue is one of four outside the Kalamazoo County Building memorializing the branches of the military. Photo by John D. Strauss

Right: Kalamazoo County is committed to support of the arts through display of public sculptures of all kinds, often coordinated by its Public Art Commission. The Fountain of the Pioneer in Bronson Park was sculpted by Chicago artist Alfonso Ianelli. Photo by John D. Strauss

Facing page below: Respected faculty, a permanent collection of some 2,000 artworks, a library, and special events throughout the year are among the offerings of the Kalamazoo Institute of Arts. Photo by Charlene Farris

presented itself, the necessary structure was in place. Money was available through generous gifts, but it was supplemented by a strong grass roots effort."

The Public Art Commission, directed by Bernard Palchick, head of the art department at Kalamazoo College, has long been promoting the concept of public art. Works by Kirk Newman and Marcia Wood adorn the landscape in front of the Art Center, in Bronson Park, at Kalamazoo College, and in front of the Kalamazoo Public Utilities Building on Stockbridge Avenue. The commission is determined that public art will become an accepted concept whenever and wherever new construction is planned.

A well-organized structure, comparable to that for public art, exists for virtually every artistic or cultural endeavor in the community. This gives the community a head start when it comes to applying for federal and state grant money. A perfect example of this is the Arts Fund of Kalamazoo, established in 1986 through a $50,000 seed-

money grant from the National Endowment for the Arts (NEA) under its program to spur community foundation initiative. The NEA's stipulation that $100,000 in matching funds must be raised from the community might have presented difficulties for other counties, but not for Kalamazoo. Through the foundations already in place, $106,000 was quickly raised, with another $10,000 pledged.

The Arts Fund, administered by the Kalamazoo Foundation, has made grants to a diverse group of artists and organizations: the Civic Black Theater, an offshoot of the Civic Players; the Mad Hatters, a theater group that promotes awareness of handicapped and disabled persons; the New Vic Theater; TABS Center, a black art and culture program presenting shows through Kalamazoo Cable Access; the Kalamazoo Concert Band; the Kalamazoo Junior Symphony; and the Friends of Poetry, a new group designed to promote local poets and the "Poetry on the Buses" contest.

Of significance is the fact that Kalamazoo is the only Michigan city to qualify for the NEA grant, and the smallest city in the program. The Kalamazoo Arts Fund is eligible for three renewals of the $50,000 grant.

A Center for the Visual Arts

The modern, well-equipped Art Center is in many ways a tribute to the efforts of the determined, dedicated individuals who worked toward its establishment for many years when facilities and funds were not so readily available. A merger of two local art clubs, the Kalamazoo Institute of Arts was incorporated in 1924—at a time when the concept of a citywide group was relatively new. In Michigan, similar groups existed only in Detroit, Grand Rapids, and Muskegon.

During the institute's early years, facilities were provided by the Board of Education and housed in a building purchased with the help of William E. Upjohn. One faction of the founding group desired a unified museum, library, and art center, and felt this concept could best be achieved through the Board of Education. The library and public museum still are funded in this way. However, another strong faction felt this concept was too limiting, suggesting "a kind of stodginess, a preoccupation with preservation and history" as opposed to "the growing edge of art."

The factional battle was a fierce one. The "growing edge" group began to win the skirmishes, but it lost the battle for a secure home. Still, although faced with a 13-year eviction notice from the Board of Education and a number of financial crises through the 1930s and 1940s, the institute continued to put together programs that more than satisfied the needs of a culture-oriented community.

The lecture series initiated in 1934 brought to Kalamazoo some of the best-known names in the art world: Diego Rivera, Thomas Hart Benton, Le Corbusier, Grant Wood, Frank Lloyd Wright, Tony Sarg, Thomas Craven, Malvina Hoffman, and Holger Cahill. Visiting instructors included Judson Smith, Alexander Brooks, George Rickey, and Philip Evergood.

In the late 1930s and early 1940s, operating on nearly nothing, the institute put together a string of exciting exhibits: Mexicans Rivera, Orozco, and Siqueiros; Chicagoans Max Weber, Francis Chapin, and Sidney Lautner; 17 paintings by Kuniyoshi; oils by Kokoschka and Philip Evergood; old masters from the Silberman Galleries; watercolors and sculptures by William Zorach, lent by the artist; paintings by Karl Hofer, the German expressionist; Coptic textiles loaned by the Los Angeles Museum of Fine Arts; and the mobiles of Alexander Calder. Many of the directors of the institute—such as Ulfert Wilke, George Rickey, Karl Priebe, and Philip Merrill—were respected artists in their own right.

By the time the institute moved into its own house on South Street in 1947, its direction and community-wide influence were solidly established—largely through the work of individuals such as Blanche Hull, first president of the institute; Mrs. William McKinley Robinson, Hull's successor; Mrs. Albert Hodgman; Lydia Siedschlag; Jane Gilmore; and George and Florence Sprau.

In 1958, the same year the Gilmore family announced plans to donate funds for a new, modern building on the South Street site, the Kalamazoo Foundation established a $500,000 endowment to finance the operations of the institute and clear the

Marcia Wood's painted steel sculpture, Procession, *stands outside the Kalamazoo Institute of Arts. The piece was created in 1985. Photo by Charlene Farris*

way for the sophisticated facility that exists today.

At the heart of the present Kalamazoo Institute of Arts is the Art Center School, a vital influence on the area's entire arts community. A respected faculty is in place, with instructors chosen on the basis of their professional training and accomplishments. The aim is to provide a high level of art experiences and training in every medium: painting/drawing, sculpture, printmaking, ceramics, photography, jewelry, and fiber. Special programs are offered for children and young adults.

The Art Center now has a permanent collection of more than 2,000 works and puts together more than 30 exhibitions each year. The exhibitions range from major shows featuring the work of internationally recognized artists to group shows focusing on regional and area artists to one-person exhibits of the work of emerging artists. Along with the permanent collection, the exhibi-

Below: A full schedule of seasonal events enriches the cultural life of Kalamazoo. Photo by John D. Strauss

The public library celebrates its own contribution to the children of Kalamazoo with this banner. Photo by John D. Strauss

tions serve a teaching function for those taking classes at the Art Center School and for the entire community.

The Art Center library has a sizable collection of books, magazines, slides, and files on all aspects of art history and art techniques. The library is open to the public, and Art Center members have book-borrowing and reference service privileges.

The Kalamazoo Institute's success in promoting a high level of art in the community is perhaps best demonstrated by the annual Bronson Park Art Fair, started in 1952 as a way of bringing art to the people through a festival atmosphere. What was then "Art on a Clothes Line" has become a major exhibit of some of the best artists in the Midwest. The Kalamazoo art fair is generally recognized as the second best of its kind in the state, after Ann Arbor.

Within the community, accomplishment in the visual arts is high. Galleries to sell local works generally have not been successful, but cooperatives such as Signature operate with a strong commitment to excellence—jurying in new members, meeting monthly, and getting together during the Christmas season to operate and staff a temporary gallery.

The Symphony: Orchestrating a Community Commitment

Even though the universities are often at the center of local initiatives to advance the arts, community involvement always reaches far beyond the walls of academia. According to Barry Ross, concert master and assistant conductor of the Kalamazoo Symphony:

We have many active, busy, important people in the community who have made a strong commitment to the arts in Kalamazoo. We have presidents of local banks, presidents and former presidents of universities, clergymen, executives of companies, and many others who give freely of their time to attend meetings and deal with matters such as programming or fund raising. That's what it takes to keep our organizations strong.

The Kalamazoo Symphony Orchestra was organized in 1921 primarily through the efforts of Leta Snow, who managed the organization for 27 years. A tireless individual, she was also instrumental in the formation of the American Symphony Orches-

tra League in 1941, now the parent organization for all symphony orchestras in the country.

Although it is not a full-time symphony—most performers are local teachers and students of music—it is one of the oldest and most respected groups of its kind in the state. "I'm a relative newcomer," said Ross. "I've been with the group only 15 years. Others have performed for 60 years or more." Yoshimi Takeda is the conductor.

The symphony is an important cultural force in Kalamazoo, with its performances in Miller Auditorium attended by loyal and enthusiastic followers. The symphony's concerts in the park each summer have created an ever-expanding audience for serious music.

The Kalamazoo Symphony Chamber Orchestra and the Bach Festival Society are offshoots of the symphony, each presenting a separate series of concerts at Kalamazoo College. The Youth Symphony concert series is held in Chenery Auditorium in the old Kalamazoo Central High School building.

Music lovers generally enjoy an embarrassment of riches in Kalamazoo County. Recitals by faculty musicians can be heard almost daily at the Dalton Center Recital Hall at Western Michigan University, and the First Presbyterian Church offers a Noon Recital Series each fall for those who work in the downtown area. The Society for Old Music concentrates on medieval and renaissance music.

Perhaps Kalamazoo is not a center for rock music, but big-name acts come with regularity to the old State Theater and to nightclubs Club Soda and Chap's on Main. In recent years artists such as Bruce Cockburn, Joan Armatrading, Emmylou Harris, Bonnie Raitt, The Nylons, and Liz Story have appeared in Kalamazoo.

Jazz, notably by Ken Morgan of Nazareth College and Bob Ricci of Western Michigan University, can be heard on a regular basis at the universities, at Tastings, Ltd., and at Chap's on Main. The Celery City Music Hall offers an excellent array of bluegrass and traditional country music at its Saturday night concerts at the Stockbridge Avenue Methodist Church.

The Stage Is a World . . .

For theater lovers, Kalamazoo offers several hundred innovative productions throughout the year: off-Broadway quality at Kalamazoo County prices.

An outgrowth of a summer stock company, the Kalamazoo Civic Players was organized in 1929 by Arthur and Francis Kohl and Norman and Louise Carver. Today James Carver is general manager of the group which has changed little over its 60-year existence.

In terms of budget, staff, and number of productions, Kalamazoo Civic is one of the largest community theaters in the country. The company employs a staff of 23 to handle production and administrative matters. Members of the production team are all experienced theater professionals, many with advanced degrees in the field. Designers work on a full-time basis providing sets, costumes, and lighting.

In addition the group takes on four interns each year, ordinarily recent college graduates who are paid a wage while they gain theater experience. Players come from a large pool of talented actors—professors, radio and TV professionals, students, and others in the community who share a semiprofessional interest in drama. Carver estimated that more than 800 volunteers contribute each year to Civic productions.

Under the rubric of the Civic Players are several production companies, all performing at the Civic Auditorium or next door at the Carver Center's theater-in-the-round: the Mainstage Theater, the Civic Youth Theater, the Civic Arena Theater, the Summer Theater, and the Black Theater. Each group operates as a separate production company, selecting its own plays, setting budgets and policies, and developing its own programs and classes. All operate with professional standards, knowing that the people of Kalamazoo take high-quality theater for granted.

Even though the Kalamazoo Civic operates as a business, ticket sales cover only 60 to 65 percent of the group's expenses. The rest comes from the community in the form of grants, gifts, and programs which tap the resources of business and industry. Through the Co-Producers Program, for example, local companies contribute several thousands of dollars toward production expenses in return for advertising, publicity, and goodwill. The sponsoring company gets top billing on the performance program and may, if it wishes, set up a booth or exhibit in the lobby. In Kalamazoo, perhaps

more than any other place, support of the arts reflects a sincere interest in the community and its development.

A more informal but no less professional theater environment is found at the New Vic. Started as a coffeehouse in 1966, New Vic Theatricals has been a labor of love for a dedicated core of actors and producers—people like Ted and Mary Jo Kistler and Arnie and Kristin Johnston. Now professional, the theater offers excellent acting and diverse shows ranging from *Bleacher Bums* to the ambitious six-hour staging of *Nicholas Nickleby*.

Loyal New Vic patrons once suffered through chilly drafts in winter and stifling heat in summer in the converted residence at the corner of Vine and John streets. Additional renovations have been made and the au-

dience can now watch in relative comfort, while sipping exotic hot or cold beverages on tables arranged on several levels around the stage.

Started in 1945, the Barn Theater is a high-level summer stock company presenting shows from late May to early September in a historical dairy barn near Augusta. Its core of Equity actors, usually including well-known stage or television artists, attracts a sizable audience from throughout the area.

Western Michigan University, Kalamazoo College, and Kalamazoo Valley Community College all have active theater programs. WMU offers a "mainstage season," with productions in the Laura Shaw Theater, plus a "black box" stage, featuring avant-garde and experimental productions in the three-quarters-round York Arena. Kala-

Above: Western Michigan University offers productions in the Laura Shaw Theater. Photo by James Riegel/The Michigan Stock Shop

Left: It may be located in an old high school building, but Chenery Auditorium has certainly presented some stellar attractions. Here, the Joffrey Ballet performs. Photo by John Gilroy/ The Michigan Stock Shop

mazoo College has a Summer Theater that blends professional and community talent, in addition to a regular offering of serious drama by students during the school year. KVCC's Ninth Street Players often presents large-scale musicals.

Smaller community groups, such as the Independent Play Producers and the Whole Art Theater, tap the county's large pool of talent and interest. The Kindleberger Summer Theater, started several years ago as part of a community festival in Parchment, is now making a significant contribution to the theater scene.

Miller Auditorium's Patron's Choice Series, at Western Michigan University, brings to the county top-quality touring shows of Broadway productions such as *Cats, Big River, La Cage Aux Folles,* and *The King and I.*

The Arts of Dance and Literature

Dance is well represented in Kalamazoo County, not only in the schools and universities but also through groups such as the Academy of Dance Arts, the Ballet Michigan Ensemble, the Kalamazoo Ballet Company, the Weaver Dance School, and the Wellspring Dance Collaborative. Wellspring, a five-member modern dance troupe, is one of the newest contributors to the arts scene in Kalamazoo.

Kalamazoo has had its share of competent poets and fiction writers. One of the most famous was novelist Edna Ferber, who was born in 1885 in a house that stood on South Park Street just opposite Ranney.

Today Western Michigan University and Kalamazoo College both have active creative writing programs, staffed by publishing writers including John Woods, Herb Scott, Conrad Hilberry, and Stuart Dybek. Both schools offer readings by nationally known poets and fiction writers, and both participate in the community-wide Poetry on the Buses program. Organized by Martha Moffett and run by the Friends of Poetry, Poetry on the Buses solicits poetry from students and residents of all ages. The best are then displayed on the city's Metro Transit buses.

Those who appreciate the arts are comfortable in Kalamazoo. Even though many larger cities might offer the same variety and level of sophistication, few communities offer as many opportunities for education and participation. The individuals who worked for decades to advance the arts and donated the money for facilities have succeeded in making the arts accessible to the people of Kalamazoo—all the while maintaining a high level of quality.

In Kalamazoo, culture is not just limited to theater and music and literature—a rich heritage of architecture is also present, as evidenced by the Frank Lloyd Wright House in Galesburg. Photo by John Gilroy/The Michigan Stock Shop

A Foundation of Education

Founded in 1903 as Western State Normal, Western Michigan University today enrolls more than 24,000 students from around the world. Photo by John Gilroy/The Michigan Stock Shop

Kalamazoo County has affirmed and reaffirmed its commitment to quality education at a number of key moments in history. This commitment dates back to the summer of 1833 when, shortly after the arrival of the first settlers, the county's first school was established in the village of Bronson (now Kalamazoo). That same year, four years before Michigan became a state, the Michigan and Huron Institute—which later became Kalamazoo College—was granted a charter. It was the first institution of higher education in the territory, and the first coeducational college in the state.

The first public high school was opened in 1858, on the site of old Kalamazoo Central on South Westnedge. Sixteen years later the "Kalamazoo decision" upheld the right of school districts in Michigan, and elsewhere, to set up free public high schools.

In 1870 Lucinda Hinsdale Stone of Kalamazoo County led the fight for the admission of women to the University of Michigan in Ann Arbor. One year later, Mary Upjohn Sidnam and Amelia Upjohn Cornell of Kalamazoo County received degrees in pharmacy from the school. Among the 10 members of the first class of women graduating after four years at the university were Ella Thomas of Schoolcraft, and Harriet Winslow and Caroline Hubbard Kleinstueck of Kalamazoo.

Caroline Bartlett Crane came to Kalamazoo in 1889 as pastor of the Unitarian Universalist People's Church, and helped create a civic educational center that included a kindergarten, a gymnasium for girls, manual training, and domestic science. These programs, highly innovative for the time, were later incorporated into the public school system and made Kalamazoo the first district in the state to offer vocational education.

To the present day, this tradition of educational leadership exerts a strong influence in Kalamazoo County.

Leading the Way in Higher Education

Through most of its history, Kalamazoo County has had more than one institution of higher education. Today it boasts a major university, two colleges, a community college, and a business college—with a combined enrollment of more than 35,000 and a faculty of more than 1,000. For the 1987-88 term, the operating budgets of the five schools surpassed $147 million—mostly spent on materials, goods, and services from Kalamazoo County.

To stress cooperation and protect diversity, in 1973 the presidents of four of the five institutions got together to form the Kalamazoo Consortium for Higher Education. Regular meetings are held to discuss issues of higher education as they affect the county. By joining together to purchase some materials and equipment, the consortium has brought about significant cost savings. Cross-registration also has allowed the five schools to make fullest use of resources without needless duplication of programs. A student at Kalamazoo Valley Community College, for example, can register at Kalamazoo College for a class not offered at KVCC.

Kalamazoo College

Kalamazoo College is a highly respected four-year liberal arts institution with an enrollment of more than 1,200. The college has grown with the city, yet a visitor could easily miss it unless he wandered onto the hilly, tree-lined campus just west of downtown Kalamazoo. Kalamazoo College never imposes itself on the community around it, yet it continues to be a vital intellectual force. Its faculty, students, and graduates are prominent participants in most cultural and artistic activities.

With a student-teacher ratio of 12-to-1, the college places a heavy emphasis on teaching. Supplementing its traditional strength in the liberal arts, the college is solidly established in math, science, preprofessional programs, economics, and business administration.

Through the unique K Plan, stu-

A Health Care County

An excellent health system like Kalamazoo County's involves much more than just hospitals: among its strengths is its highly sophisticated trauma network which transports patients from a 10-county radius to whatever facility may be appropriate. Borgess Inflight Medical Service is one of the most impressive links in the network, along with Bronson Care-Flite. Photo by John Gilroy/The Michigan Stock Shop

After arriving in Richland in 1836, Dr. Uriah Upjohn practiced medicine for 45 years—riding on horseback throughout the county to deliver care, often to rural people too poor to pay. As a physician, he clearly did not make a fortune; yet, of his 12 children, 11 survived to adulthood and 5 went on to gain degrees from the medical school at the University of Michigan. Mary and Amelia Upjohn were the university's first women graduates in pharmacy; Helen, Henry U., and William E. Upjohn earned M.D. degrees. William E. would later found The Upjohn Company—now a *Fortune* 500 company and a health care leader throughout the world.

Orthopedic surgeon Dr. Homer Stryker, working out of a basement room at Borgess Medical Center 100 years after Uriah Upjohn's arrival, produced a series of important medical innovations. In 1936 he invented the Stryker turning frame for moving patients with spinal injuries. He later patented the practical rubber heel for the bottom of walking casts, a nailing board for hip fractures, an over-the-bed frame to support limbs in traction, and a grasping bar to enable bedridden patients to move themselves. In 1942 he produced an oscillating saw for physicians to use to cut through casts without injuring the flesh beneath.

The Stryker Corporation, founded in 1946, now employs more than 500 persons in Kalamazoo County. Its activities include the manufacturing and worldwide marketing of a broad line of surgical instruments, operating room devices, cast cutters, and other equipment for the handling, treatment, and care of patients.

Upjohn and Stryker are only two of the many physicians who have left their mark on Kalamazoo. The first postmaster of the village of Bronson, appointed in 1832, was Dr. Jonathan Abbott; the first city bacteriologist and a pioneer in the field of radiology was Dr. Augustus Crane, husband of educational reformer Caroline Bartlett Crane; and one of the early leaders in neuro-surgery was Dr. Richard Upjohn Light. A great-grandson of Uriah Upjohn, Light invented a device to electrically stimulate an animal's nervous system by remote control—an innovation that eventually led to the development of the cardiac pacemaker. Later, as a research scientist at The Upjohn Company, Light was instrumental in the testing and development of Gelfoam, a gelatin sponge used to control bleeding during brain surgery.

The first state psychiatric hospital was established in Kalamazoo in 1853, made possible through the efforts of citizens who vigorously campaigned for it, donated land, and raised funds for its construction. It was a radical idea in an era when many considered mental illness an embarrassment, if not a crime. In the twentieth century the state hospital has been joined by two regional medical centers: Bronson Methodist Hospital and Borgess Medical Center.

Today Kalamazoo has a medical community of about 500 practicing physicians—not including many persons with M.D. and Ph.D. degrees employed in research at The Upjohn Company and the Stryker Corporation—who cover the complete spectrum of specialties and subspecialties. A highly sophisticated trauma network, including two helicopters, transports patients from a 10-county radius to the most appropriate level of care.

Four of the county's 10 major employers—employing more than 12,500 persons—deliver some kind of health care service or product. Drawing on a strong tradition, Kalamazoo is, as many say, a "health care county."

Bill Burian, Ph.D., who died in 1988, served admirably as dean of the College of Health and Human Services at Western Michigan University and president of the Southwest Michigan Health Coordinating Council. Burian was suitably proud of the health care delivery network he helped coordinate. "I think the people of this area are very well served," he said. "For a county this size, Kalamazoo has an extremely sophisticated health care system."

In recent years, Borgess Medical Center has brought the era of specialized medicine to Kalamazoo County. Photo by John Gilroy/The Michigan Stock Shop

As Burian pointed out, "the two hospitals are excellent, both tertiary centers of equal strength with complementary areas of specialization." The two hospitals have been highly competitive over the past several decades, but Burian and the Southwest Michigan Health Coordinating Council were sucessful in bringing them closer together. In late 1987 the presidents of the two institutions announced a move to work together in a number of areas to better serve the needs of the community. As Burian stated:

Our two hospitals are not simply Kalamazoo hospitals. They are regional medical centers, and they must continue to be. For the future, the important issue is not competition between Borgess and Bronson—because we need them both—but rather competition between our hospitals and those from other cities such as Ann Arbor, Grand Rapids, South Bend, Toledo, and even Chicago and Detroit.

Borgess Medical Center

Borgess Medical Center was the county's first hospital, started in 1889 by Father Francis A. O'Brien, St. Augustine parish priest, and operated by the Sisters of St. Joseph in a converted house in downtown Kalamazoo. Their goal was to provide care for the sick and homeless, and their mission of healing

has been maintained through the years as Borgess has evolved from a small community hospital into a major regional medical center. Each year a large number of patients receive some kind of charity care, and the hospital works to ensure that all persons in the community have access to good medical care.

Borgess was still a small community hospital when Martin Verzi came to head the medical center in July 1966, after 20 years with the U.S. Army medical service. Now retired and a consultant to a number of institutions, Verzi described the situation at Borgess upon his arrival:

In the last two decades, Kalamazoo's medical facilities have fully arrived in the era of specialized medicine. Patients arrive from all over the region to undergo advanced surgical procedures such as kidney transplants and open-heart surgery in the operating rooms of Borgess Medical Center. Photo by John Gilroy/The Michigan Stock Shop

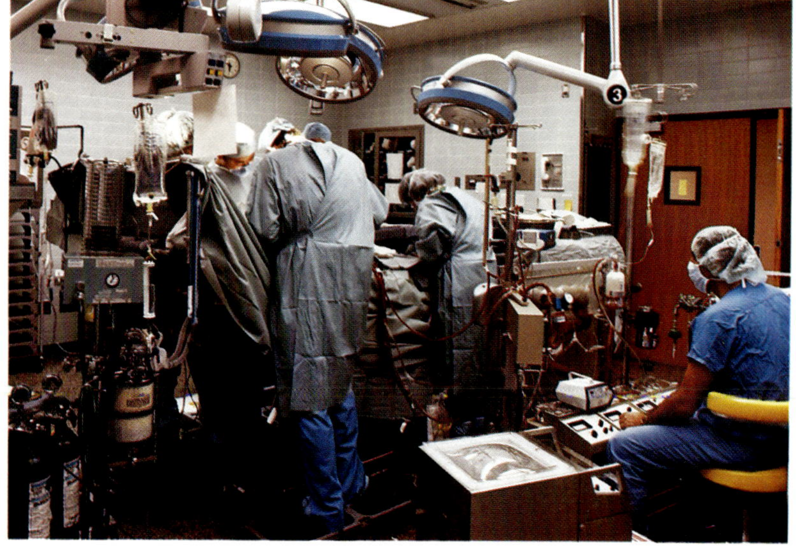

Bronson [
tal has st
for famil
nity care
the full r
pregancio
Photo by
The Mic

Another facility that draws patients to Kalamazoo for specialized treatment is the Cardiac Rehabilitation Institute. Photo by John Gilroy/ The Michigan Stock Shop

The time was right. Ten days after I arrived in town, Medicare was enacted, and the federal government began to single out heart disease, cancer, stroke, and kidney disease as major killers. The resources and technology were available; the Sisters of St. Joseph and the Board of Trustees made the commitment to build an up-to-date medical center; and those were the programs we outlined for Borgess—heart, stroke, cancer, and kidney. We already had a good mental health program, and it was being expanded through money donated by Dorothy Dalton. But there was no alcoholism treatment, and that was another major killer.

In the two decades that followed, Borgess and its rival hospital across town brought the era of specialized medicine to Kalamazoo County. Neurology required neurosurgery, cardiology required cardiac surgery, a good cancer program required a full complement of support services, and the kidney program led to hemodialysis and kidney transplantation. Mental health services were expanded, and an alcoholism treatment center was created. All required state-of-the-art equipment, laboratory, and research facilities, and highly trained nursing, laboratory, and support personnel.

Borgess Medical Center now has one of the most comprehensive heart care programs in the Midwest. Its staff of specialized cardiologists and cardiac surgeons includes top names in the field, recruited from major research centers and hospitals. Cardiac surgery was initiated as early as 1972, and the medical center still has the only comprehensive open-heart surgery facility in the

area. The Cardiovascular Laboratory ranks high in terms of number of procedures performed and breadth of services offered. By mid-1987, cardiologists at Borgess had performed more than 3,598 angioplasty procedures, placing the medical center among the best in the world for this technique.

For postsurgical and heart attack patients, Borgess offers specialized intensive care units, well equipped and staffed by highly experienced nurses. The Cardiovascular Institute provides long-term rehabilitation for heart attack patients and preventive monitoring of the cardiovascular health of the community. Located in a separate building behind the hospital, it was the first hospital-affiliated unit of its kind in the country.

Dr. Richard Upjohn Light established an early tradition in neurosurgery in Kalamazoo, but a sensitive skin condition forced him to leave surgical practice in 1946 for a career in experimental science at The Upjohn Company. The vacuum in that area went largely unfilled until neurologist Russell Mohney, M.D., and neurosurgeon Robert Fabi, M.D., arrived in Kalamazoo from the Mayo Clinic to establish what has become one of the most comprehensive, integrated neurology programs in the area. A team of highly respected neurology and neurosurgical specialists now operates out of the Kalamazoo Neurological Institute, a diagnostic/research center that houses the first Magnetic Resonance Imaging equipment in this part of the state. This team also has access to other up-to-date diagnostic tools, including CT scans, EEG, EMG, and digital subtraction angiography.

Borgess' Neuro Intensive Care Unit was the first of its kind in the state (others today are in Ann Arbor, Lansing, and Saginaw). It is staffed by specially trained intensive care nurses and equipped with the most up-to-date monitoring equipment. As an adjunct, Borgess recently initiated a Spinal Injury Center for treatment of all aspects of spinal cord and head injuries. Borgess also offers a strong nephrology program (for the study and treatment of kidney disorders) and has the only kidney transplantation facilities in southwest Michigan.

Constructed in 1917, the present hospital structure on Gull Road underwent major renovation and rebuilding in 1987 to provide the facilities needed for a modern tertiary care center.

Bronson

Bronson M
ilar to the
cember 4
formed w
tal Assoc
from loca
12-bed h
tal was re
ter the ci
Bronson.
john cha
ney for a
the prese
downtov
filiated v
Church
to reflec

Ever
111-bed
convales
and agai
tal laun
tion pro
extensiv
paigns.

To
cilities
and for
nancies
tensive
southw
lifesavir
by a hi
cial Ba
with th
transpo
commi

Th
childre
also ta
a chee
24-hor
rics In
vides
Bi
adults
intens
follow
staff is
ical ar
seriou
nying
lems.
E
which

weeks of intensive inpatient treatment, designed to help them learn to manage pain
by reactivating their bodies' natural pain-
killers. The program involves counseling, exer-
cise, biofeedback training, and physical
therapy.

Alcoholism and Other Drug Dependencies

For the treatment of alcoholism and other
drug dependencies, the Midwest Recovery
Center at Borgess offers a number of treatment options for both adults and adoles-
cents. The center is particularly strong in
its ability to evaluate and assess individuals, as-
signing each to an appropriate level of treatment. Although some can be treated as
outpatients, others require intensive treatment in the hospital.

All primary therapists at the Midwest Recovery Center have at least a master's degree, plus a specialization in substance
abuse. Most are licensed psychologists with
a specialization in addiction therapy. The
ratio of five patients to each primary therapist is excellent, far exceeding the state
requirement of no more than 10 patients
per primary therapist.

The Kalamazoo Area Drug Abuse Coun-

*Above: Kalamazoo Re-
gional Psychiatric Hospi-
tal, formerly Kalamazoo
State Hospital, has a
long history of providing
high-quality services for
adults and children.
Photo by John A. Lacko/
The Michigan Stock
Shop*

*Left: A therapist works
with a young patient at
the Constance Brown
Hearing and Speech Cen-
ter at Western Michigan
University. The univer-
sity also has programs
for the rehabilitation of
the blind. Photo by John
Gilroy/The Michigan
Stock Shop*

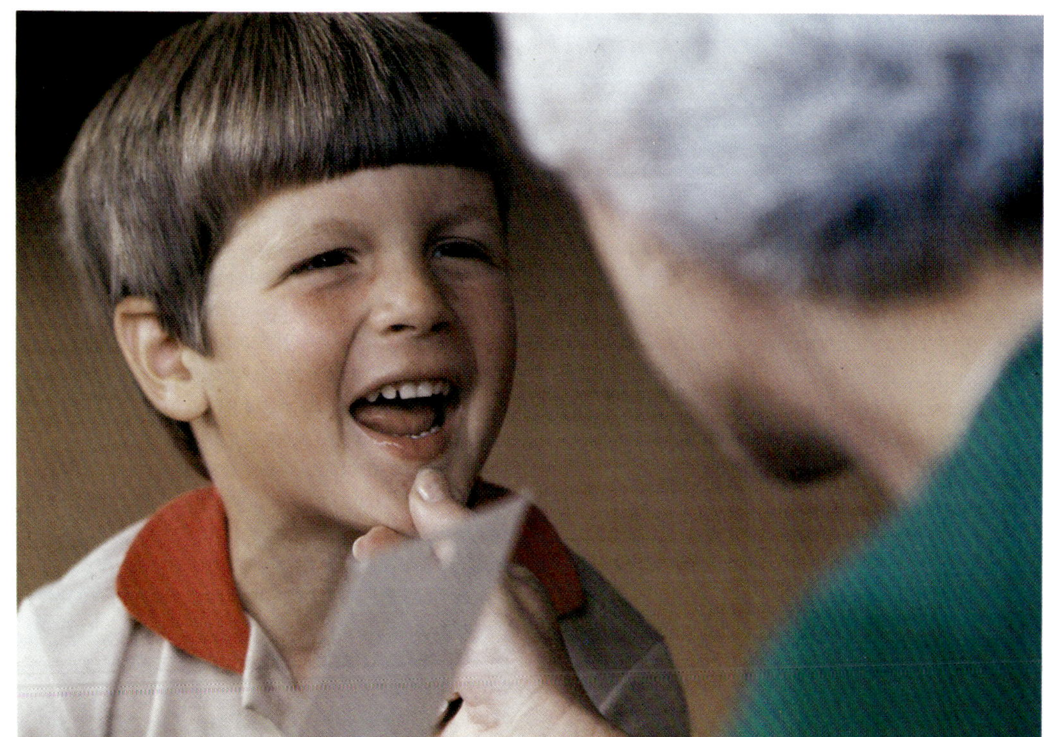

cil, a nonprofit organization, provides educational and counseling services, runs successful youth and parent programs, and operates a 24-hour crisis line.

Specialized Services

Geriatric programs are offered by both hospitals to complement the excellent network of programs operated by Senior Services. Upjohn HealthCare Services and the Visiting Nurse Association provide home health care services, and CareTec supplies equipment such as respirators and wheelchairs for care in the home. An excellent nursing home system—with a range of options—exists for those who need long-term care; private apartment complexes provide social opportunities for those who can live independently with a limited amount of monitoring and assistance.

Self-help and support groups have been established for chronic diseases such as Alzheimer's, Parkinson's, cerebral palsy, Down's syndrome, multiple sclerosis, muscular dystrophy, myasthenia gravis, myelodysplasia, and spina bifida. Other groups provide support for those suffering from apnea, epilepsy, speech impairments, and hyperactivity. Bronson/Vicksburg hospital has good facilities for the rehabilitation of stroke patients and those suffering serious head and neurological injuries. The Center for Independent Living and the Borgess Back-to-Work Center provide services to help many of these disabled persons work their way back into the mainstream.

Other specialized services in the community include the Michigan Rehabilitation Center for the Blind and the Constance Brown Hearing and Speech Center at Western Michigan University.

Access for All a Priority

Nationally as well as locally, access to quality health care has become a major issue. Studies show that even with the growth of sophisticated health services and facilities, increasing numbers of persons do not have access to the care they need. Medical indigents include not only the unemployed and homeless but also those who are underemployed or underinsured.

Access is a problem that many individuals and communities would like to ignore—but not Kalamazoo County. A tradition was established during the days of Dr. Uriah Upjohn, and it is strongly supported by the county's major health care institutions and organizations. In Kalamazoo County, good health care for all is a high priority.

A well-developed regional trauma network includes personnel in the field and at area hospitals, several ambulance services, and two helicopters to transport critically ill or injured patients. Photo by John Gilroy/The Michigan Stock Shop

Taking It Easy

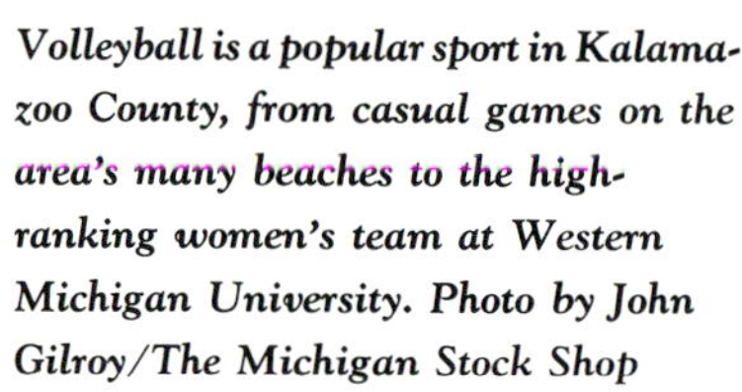

Volleyball is a popular sport in Kalamazoo County, from casual games on the area's many beaches to the high-ranking women's team at Western Michigan University. Photo by John Gilroy/The Michigan Stock Shop

For nearly every mood or occasion, there's a little bit of green space—or white, as the case may be—in Kalamazoo County. From Gull Lake on the north to Indian Lake on the south, the area is dotted with lakes, parks, ponds, and meadows—many tucked away behind shopping or living centers and known only to the initiated.

Asylum Lake, a 240-acre reserve within the Kalamazoo city limits, is a perfect example, found by following a path at the end of Winchell Street or off Drake Road or Parkview Street. Only a few steps away from a comfortable suburban neighborhood, Asylum Lake is a pocket of wilderness. Paths wind through forested areas, strewn with wild raspberry bushes and wildflowers. There are small beaches around the lake but no manicured picnic areas . . . and no crowds. On weekends one might see a fisherman in a rowboat or canoe out in the middle of the reed-filled lake; in late afternoon one might see joggers or a school cross-country team working out on the hilly paths. Ordinarily, however, a person can feel that he has the whole area pretty much to himself.

The area was once part of the Kalamazoo State Hospital, operated as a dairy farm by psychiatric patients. In the 1960s the buildings were torn down and the land was turned over to Western Michigan University. Today powerboats and motorcycles are banned from the lake. Foxes, deer, raccoons, and other wildlife find refuge in the wooded areas and on the rolling pastures and prairie land.

Ducks, swans, and several bands of Canada geese make either permanent or winter homes at several sites in Kalamazoo County: Asylum Lake, the Crosstown Ponds area near downtown Kalamazoo, Kleinstuck Marsh behind the Kalamazoo Family YMCA, Gourdneck State Game Area in Portage, Fred McLinden Park on Campbell Lake in Comstock, Kellogg Bird Sanctuary, the Kalamazoo Nature Center in Cooper Township, and various areas scattered throughout the county. In autumn, urban residents often experience the thrill of seeing a flock of geese take to the sky, circle in formation, and then land again with a whirring, honking commotion.

Green Space at the Center: Bronson Park

The green space at the center of Kalamazoo is Bronson Park. In 1831 Titus Bronson, founder and developer of the city of Kalamazoo, donated four squares of land in the center of the village for public use: one for a courthouse, another for a jail, a third for an academy, and a fourth for a cluster of churches. The jail and the academy have since been moved but the courthouse and the churches remain, and the park in the middle is the symbolic heart of the county.

Officially set aside as a park in the late 1840s, Bronson Park is county land, leased to the city for one dollar a year. The current 50-year lease dates back to 1964. Abraham Lincoln, Stephen Douglas, Theodore Roosevelt, and William Jennings Bryan spoke near the grassy mound that is believed to date back to the time of the Hopewell Indians. Mourners for the slain Martin Luther King, Jr., rallied there under oak trees that predate the coming of settlers to the area. Today a place where shoppers can rest for a few minutes beside the fountain or downtown workers can have a leisurely brown-bag lunch, the park is the site of most major festivals, shows, fairs, and political rallies.

A juried art fair sponsored by the Kalamazoo Institute of Arts is held at the park each year among the permanent works of public art that have been erected there reflecting the history of the community. *The Fountain of the Pioneer*, sculpted by Alfonso Ianelli of Chicago, created some controversy when it was unveiled in 1940. Depicting an armed pioneer pushing an Indian chief, it retells all too clearly a story many would like to forget—of Potawatomi Indians being forced from their homeland and sent packing to reservations in the west.

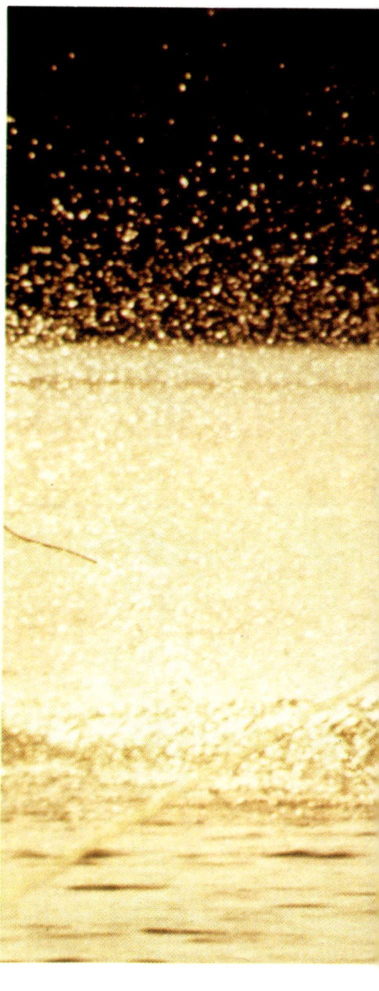

Top left: Overlooking Wintergreen Lake, the Kellogg Bird Sanctuary has earned a national reputation for its contributions to wildlife management and environmental education. The sanctuary provides refuge for a variety of North American birds. Photo by John D. Strauss

Left: Dancers perform at a Bronson Park fiesta. The Hispanic festival is just one of many ethnic celebrations that take place regularly in Kalamazoo County. Photo by Charlene Farris

site of many city sporting events. Tucked behind businesses—visible only during the winter months when the trees are barren—is Woods Lake beach, a favorite summer haunt for youngsters. And across from Mount EverRest Cemetery on South Burdick is parkland donated from the estate of Blanche Hull, a prominent figure in the cultural history of the community. Behind the old Hull estate is Monarch Mill Pond, another little-known preserve for lovers of birds, plants, and wildflowers.

Parchment has an expansive and immaculately kept family park named after the founder of the KVP Company, Jacob Kindleberger. It is the site each year of the Kindleberger Summer Festival.

Most of the other parks in the county are located in scenic areas near lakes or along the riverbank: Ramona Park, Lakeview Park, and West Lake Nature Preserve in Portage; Prairieview Park near Schoolcraft and Vicksburg; Coldbrook Park near Climax; River Oaks Park between Comstock and Galesburg; and El Sabo Preserve near Kalamazoo Valley Community College in Oshtemo. A historic gristmill can be observed at Scotts Mill Park near Scotts.

The Rites of Spring Valley

Spring Valley Park, surrounding Spring Valley Lake in a basin of the Kalamazoo River behind Borgess Medical Center and Nazareth College, is the site each April of what has become a rite of spring—Borgess Medical Center's "Run for the Health of It." More than 5,000 runners and countless spectators gather for a number of events: 15-kilometer, 10-kilometer, and 5-kilometer runs (including wheelchair competition); a 5-kilometer walk; and a "medical mile" that brings together physicians, nurses, and cardiac rehabilitation patients. One of the largest road races in Michigan, the Run for the Health of It has become much more than a running competition. Held on what is usually one of the first really warm days of spring, it is an occasion for runners, spectators, and friends to soak up the sun and eat a picnic lunch together on the grass overlooking the lake.

The second leg of Kalamazoo's unofficial "triple crown" of racing is the "Beech Leaf Run" : 5- and 10-kilometer races held in May on the hilly, tree-lined trails of the Kalamazoo Nature Center. The third leg, sched-

uled in mid-June, is the Kalamazoo Track Club's "Kalamazoo Klassic." Runners in these 5- and 10-kilometer events start at the Kalamazoo Family YMCA and wind their way through one of the city's most pleasant neighborhoods.

The Track Club also promotes running and wellness through low-key events, held nearly every week during the running season. Larger competitions in the area include the Gull Lake Triathlon, the Hickory Corners Biathlon (running and biking), the Great Paper Chase at Western Michigan University, the Plainwell Classic, and the Peacock Strut sponsored by the Portage City on the Grow Committee. The latter event, held in the fall, is run on country roads and suburban drives in the fast-growing area of west Portage and finishes at the Centre Court Health Club.

In the winter, runners gather for smaller running events: the West Hills Athletic Club's Run and Chill and the annual New Year's Day fiasco, the 1/1 Run, sponsored by the Gazelle Sporting Goods store and held on the snowy paths of Spring Valley Park.

For the most part, Kalamazoo County is usually under a fairly heavy cover of snow from December through February— creating ideal conditions for cross-country skiing in most of the parks mentioned above.

Downhill skiers can choose from three areas in the near vicinity and many more within a five-hour drive. To the northwest, near Plainwell and Otsego, are the Timber Ridge Ski Area and Bittersweet Ski Resort. To the southwest, near Marcellus, is the Swiss Valley Ski Area. All three have good chair lifts and several ski runs geared to all skill levels.

Spectator Sports

Since 1973 spectators have enjoyed professional hockey at Kalamazoo's Wings Stadium. The K-Wings of the International Hockey League are now a primary development club for the Minnesota North Stars, after serving as a secondary club for Detroit, Philadelphia, and Vancouver. Players assigned to Kalamazoo are, for the most part, top prospects just out of university or junior hockey, vying for an opportunity to make the National Hockey League club. Directing the Wings' operations is a board that includes R. Ted Parfet, Martha Parfet, and Jim Gilmore, Jr.

Milham Park, a favorite site for family outings, delights children with a brook and waterfowl. Photo by John Gilroy/ The Michigan Stock Shop

Many members of the Kalamazoo Wings, an International Hockey League team, are hot prospects for the NHL. The local ice arena is quick to fill up with fans when the home team shows off its moves. Photo by John Gilroy/The Michigan Stock Shop

Echo Valley Winter Sports Park, just minutes north of downtown Kalamazoo, offers a spacious skating rink and thrilling toboggan rides at speeds approaching 60 miles per hour. Photo by John D. Strauss

Motor sports are also strong in the area, with top competition at the Martin U.S. 131 Dragway north of Kalamazoo, the Kalamazoo Speedway, and the Galesburg Speedway.

Western Michigan University's sports teams compete in the strong Mid-American Conference. The Broncos have won two national championships in men's cross-country running, and the women's volleyball team has ranked among the top 20 teams in the country several times over the last decade.

Kalamazoo College competes against Alma, Albion, Adrian, Hope, Calvin, and Olivet colleges in the Michigan Intercollegiate Athletic Association. From 1985 to 1987, the Hornets reigned as national champions in NCAA Division III tennis.

Nazareth, expanding and improving its sports programs for men and women, recently built a new indoor facility for volleyball and basketball. The Moles compete against a national group of small-enrollment schools in the Little Colleges Athletic Association.

Kalamazoo Valley Community College has won state championships in men's basket-

Along with Michigan as a whole, Kalamazoo County shares a keen interest in cars. Classic auto shows take place in the summer, and for those who crave action there are plenty of motor sports events. The Martin U.S. 131 Dragway is just one of three major racetracks in the area. Photos by John D. Strauss

ball and tennis. Its women's softball team has earned national rankings for several years in a row.

A County for Athletes

Among tennis enthusiasts, Kalamazoo has long had a national reputation as host to the U.S. Tennis Association's Boys' 16-18 National Tennis Tournament. Since 1943 hundreds of the best young players in the country have descended upon Kalamazoo College each August for nine days of intense competition. Those who have competed in past years include Arthur Ashe, Marty Riessen, Ray Senkowski, Aaron Krickstein, and John McEnroe. In recent years a Celebrity Warm-Up has been scheduled for the Thursday before competition begins, pairing Junior Davis Cup players with members of the media in amateur and professional doubles divisions.

Kalamazoo also hosts the Little League Softball World Series each year at the Milwood playing field complex. As with the tennis tournament, the community provides the volunteer support needed to handle the logistics and crowds of a national event.

More than a thousand men and women in the county participate in team sports activities through their employers and city leagues. And for young people, the county has a wealth of well-organized sports activities.

The fastest growing of these is soccer, attracting more than 7,500 in the area to its various programs. The American Youth Soccer Organization plays at a 10-field complex off of Drake Road; the Michigan Independent Soccer League has a six-field complex in Portage. In winter months, "Kick N Around" indoor play is available off East Kilgore Road.

Rocket football is strong in Portage, drawing more than a thousand 8- to 15-year-old boys to its Saturday matches. The Kalamazoo Kayo Club holds wrestling and boxing competitions. Other organized sports activities include Small Fry and Youth basketball; Little League, Connie Mack, and Mickey Mantle baseball; Tee-ball (for 5- to 10-year-old boys and girls); and Mite, Squirt, Peewee, and Bantam hockey leagues. The YMCA offers programs in judo, karate, swimming, gymnastics, volleyball, and basketball. The more talented girls in volleyball participate in the Kalamazoo Juniors program.

For adult men and women, one of the

Kalamazoo boasts a wide variety of organized sports leagues for young people, such as the Optimist hockey club shown here. Photo by John Gilroy/The Michigan Stock Shop

top competitive events of the year is the YMCA Community Corporate Olympics. More than 4,000 employees of corporations operating in the county compete in running, biking, swimming, and cheerleading events held each September at Western Michigan University, Kalamazoo College, and Spring Valley Park. Stressing fitness and good health, the Corporate Olympics program includes fitness testing and training seminars to help participants prepare themselves for competition.

Other Leisure Pursuits

For less organized fitness and recreation, county residents have the Kalamazoo Family YMCA, the new YWCA in downtown Kalamazoo, and numerous fitness centers, health clubs, and racquet clubs in the area. With 83 lakes, 2 rivers, and dozens of streams, there is ample opportunity for sailing, powerboating, canoeing, water skiing, swimming, and fishing for pike, bass, and trout. In the fall the area has good hunting grounds for geese, ducks, pheasants, and deer. Ice fishing is a favorite winter activity.

For golfers there are good courses—municipal, public, and private—in all parts of the county.

Municipal courses include:

*Eastern Hills on Gull Road (27 holes: 18 holes, par 72; west 9, par 36; motorized carts)

*Milham Park on Lovers Lane (18 holes, par 72; no motorized carts)

*Red Arrow on King Highway (executive 9 holes, par 29)

Public courses include:

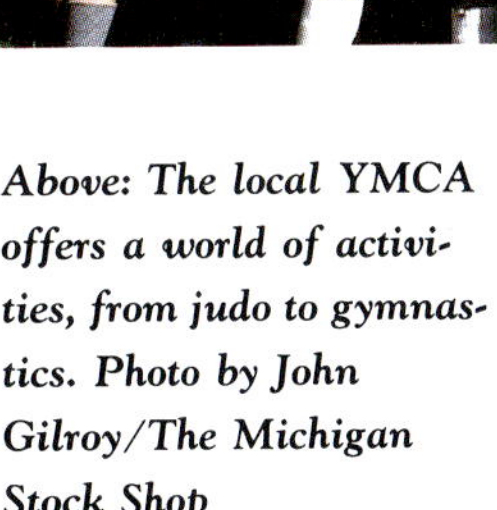

Above: The local YMCA offers a world of activities, from judo to gymnastics. Photo by John Gilroy/The Michigan Stock Shop

Top right: Kalamazoo is a haven for anglers, who test their skills in the area's numerous streams and lakes which afford a mouth-watering assortment of game fish. Photo by John D. Strauss

Right: A tuba concert adds something marvelously different to this New Year's celebration at city hall. Photo by John A. Lacko/The Michigan Stock Shop

*Crestview, D Avenue near Parchment (18 holes, par 72; motorized carts)

*Grand Prairie, 3620 Grand Prairie in Oshtemo (executive 9 holes, par 30)

*Gull Lake View, M-89 in Richland (36 holes, both par 72; motorized carts; dining facilities)

*Indian Run, Scotts (18 holes, par 72; motorized carts; dining facilities)

*Lake Doster, M-89 near Richland (18 holes, par 72; motorized carts; dining facilities)

*Maple Hills, 16344 East C Avenue (9 holes, par 36; motorized carts)

*Oakland Hills, 8716 Oakland Drive (9 holes, par 36; motorized carts)

*Ridgeview, M-43 west (18 holes: regulation 9, executive 9; motorized carts; dining facilities)

*States, 20 East W Avenue, Vicksburg (18 holes, par 72; motorized carts; dining facilities)

*Thornapple Creek, 6415 West F Avenue (18 holes, par 72; motorized carts; dining facilities)

Private courses include:

*Kalamazoo Country Club, Whites Road (18 holes, par 72; executive 9)

*Elks Country Club, West Main and U.S. 131 in Oshtemo (18 holes, par 72)

*Gull Lake Country Club, Gull Lake

Drive in Richland
(18 holes, par 72)
   *The Moors,
3810 West Center
in Portage (18
holes, par 72)

Farmers' Market, Festivals, and Fairs

Started in 1947 and open three days a week during the growing season, the Bank Street Farmers' Market is a social gathering spot as well as a place to buy fresh fruits and vegetables, honey, eggs, fresh-dressed chickens, baked goods, green plants, and flower baskets. Sellers from Kalamazoo County and the neighboring counties of Allegan, Barry, Berrien, Branch, Calhoun, Cass, Eaton, St. Joseph, and Van Buren rent spaces and bring to market a harvest of fruits and vegetables from the fertile growing area. During the strawberry season each year, the Farmers' Market hosts a Strawberry Festival—offering numerous ways to enjoy the fresh flavor of this prolific fruit.

Festivals and fairs are big in Kalamazoo County. The area's rich ethnic heritage is celebrated through a Greek Festival, a Spanish Fiesta, a German Oktoberfest, and a Children's One World Festival. The annual art fair has become a major gathering place, not only for those included in the invitational show in Bronson Park but for others who set up booths in the downtown mall and along streets near the city center.

Other festivals include the Bronson Methodist Hospital Family Health Fair, the Kazoo School Fair, the Portage City on the Grow celebration, the Antique Automobile Festival in Vicksburg, the Lions Club Chicken Barbecue in Richland, and the Festival of Flour at Scotts Mill County Park. Tours of historic homes are held in Kalamazoo and Plainwell. The Kalamazoo Nature Center holds a Harvest Fest, a Maple Sugaring Weekend, and a Christmas at DeLano Homestead celebration. The county fair is held each August at the fairgrounds east of Kalamazoo.

A String of Special Events

Three of the largest special events—the air show, the Flowerfest, and the Wine and Harvest Festival—provide action during June, July, and September.

Started in 1981 as an air show and

open house sponsored by the city of Kalamazoo and the Kalamazoo County Chamber of Commerce, the Michigan International Air Show—High on Kalamazoo has become a major event held each June. More than 100,000 spectators watch dazzling performances by classic and antique planes and demonstrations by some of the most advanced military craft in existence. Airborne stunt teams and wingwalkers are regulars on the program. A Fair Share Air Fair, held in conjunction with the air show, brings several hundred companies from across the country to meet with local manufacturers and suppliers and highlights the assets and resources available in Kalamazoo County.

Celebrating the county's status as the nation's largest producer of bedding plants, the Flowerfest brings a burst of color to Kalamazoo each July. The festival includes a flower show, outdoor concerts, book sales, art displays, and walking tours to appreciate the flowers that bloom on Library Lane in Portage, in Bronson and Crane Parks in Kalamazoo, and throughout the county. In 1988 a three-dimensional peacock, 12 feet in height and made of flowers, decorated the west end of Bronson Park. In addition to receiving write-ups in national publications, the Flowerfest has inspired similar celebrations in other parts of the state and country.

One of the largest producers of wine in Michigan and the fourth-largest wine-growing area in the country, southwest Michigan is home each September to the Wine and Harvest Festival. Presenting their wines for tasting at the annual event are wineries such as Warner, St. Julian, Bronte, and Frontenac from Paw Paw; Tabor Hill and Lemon Creek from Berrien Springs; and Fenn Valley from Fennville. More than 200,000 persons flock to Kalamazoo and Paw Paw to tour the wineries, sample ethnic foods, and take part in activities ranging from grape stomping to bed racing.

For artisans, entrepreneurs, and restaurateurs, all of these events offer rich opportunities to reach the public. For residents, they are additional ways to take it easy and celebrate life in Kalamazoo County.

Above & facing page: The Michigan International Air Show—High on Kalamazoo draws some 100,000 spectators each time its dazzling display of skill and technology takes to the air. Airborne stunts and unusual aircraft—the old, the flashy, and the amazing ultra-new—are the main attractions. Concurrently, the Fair Share Air Fair gives local manufacturers and suppliers a chance to do business with companies from across the nation. Photos by John A. Lacko/The Michigan Stock Shop and John D. Strauss

These "Volunteens," shown at Cheff Center, an equestrian facility for the handicapped, are a segment of the United Way's effort to recruit volunteers of all ages to serve community needs. Here, handicapped youths are treated to horseback rides as recreational therapy. Photo by John Gilroy/ The Michigan Stock Shop

With a stable population, a strong industrial base, and an employment rate consistently higher than state and national averages, Kalamazoo County has in the past seldom needed to aggressively court new industry the way some communities have. Looking to the future, however, the county is determined not to let past success lead it into a false sense of security.

In an era of increasingly stiff competition for new jobs, the Kalamazoo County Economic Expansion Corporation (KCEEC) was established in 1975 as a nonprofit organization to conduct an aggressive program of economic growth. While KCEEC performed admirably over the years in retaining old and attracting new employers, the group's board of directors felt the need for a comprehensive long-range strategy.

Started in 1988 as an offshoot of KCEEC, the Kalamazoo County CEO Council is the brainchild of a top-level study of the county's strengths and needs conducted by a coalition of business, education, and government leaders. The plan, as recommended by this study, is to act from a position of strength—when the economy was already generating many new jobs each month—in developing and implementing an aggressive plan for the future. Shifting the financial burden for economic development from the public to the private sector, the plan calls upon those who best know the needs of business—other business leaders—to coordinate and lead the effort.

The CEO Council consists of 16 leaders—primarily from business, education, and foundations—who have already demonstrated the ability and the commitment to build a better Kalamazoo County. The organization is directed by a professional economic developer. Working closely with development specialists from each of the individual cities and townships of the county—but clearly separate from any political or jurisdictional entity—the CEO Council now serves as the primary countywide economic development agency. Its mission is to build upon existing strengths in developing the area's human, technical, and capital resources.

The CEO Council is committed to accomplishing the following goals by the end of its fifth year:

1. *Establish a research/business park.*

2. *Develop an incubator for start-up businesses.*

3. *Add 20,000 new jobs, of which approximately half will be the result of attracting new employers.*

4. *Assemble a land bank controlled by the agency.*

5. *Increase personal and business income levels.*

6. *Ensure the long-term viability of an economic expansion effort directed by the private sector.*

Within this time frame, the council hopes to establish itself as a workable model for economic development agencies throughout the country.

Building from Strength

Those who already live and work in Kalamazoo County know that the area offers cultural and recreational facilities ordinarily found only in much larger cities. One man who was forced to take a job in Milwaukee comes back to Kalamazoo every weekend. Active in the symphony and other community activities, the man said: "I won't leave, and my wife won't think of leaving."

Ranking high among the county's assets—and often underrated—are its excellent educational resources. With good school systems, a university, and four colleges, the county offers not only a well-educated labor pool but also a number of specific resources and services.

Through the years, the private and public sectors have cooperated in supporting and enhancing these cultural, educational, and recreational facilities. As the

The Upjohn Company's Asgrow agricultural chemical facility is located on the highway midway between Comstock and Richland. Photos by John Gilroy/The Michigan Stock Shop

In providing for human services, Kalamazoo County has always relied heavily on the social concerns of its religious institutions. More than 200 established churches representing about 50 denominations exist in the county. Photo by John D. Strauss

For more than a decade, concerned members of the community have worked for a wastewater treatment system capable of restoring the river as a source of community pride. Photo by John A. Lacko/The Michigan Stock Shop

Drawing on a strong tradition, Kalamazoo is, as many say, a "health care county." Photo by John Gilroy/The Michigan Stock Shop

that other methods cannot handle successfully. Highly effective with complex industrial as well as organic wastes, the method has been installed in several large industrial plants but only a handful of municipal facilities. Officials say it provides the highest level of treatment possible rather than merely the level required by state and federal governments.

The entire system is computer-controlled, with a professional staff monitoring and evaluating what goes into and out of the system 24 hours a day, 7 days a week. A field laboratory crew draws water samples from throughout the city and at various industrial sites to be analyzed in the lab. Another crew goes out by boat to take samples from representative locations on the river. In the lab, tests are run for phosphorus, trace metals, bacteria, volatile organic chemicals, and other substances. Additional teams work with local industries on special problems.

For companies considering Kalamazoo County as a site for relocation, the Water Reclamation Facility is ideal for filling virtually any industrial need. In the words of one of its consulting engineers: "If this plant can't

treat an industrial waste, no plant can. I know of no other municipality that offers better treatment." An added advantage is that public officials at the local level take responsibility for monitoring, evaluation, government liaison, and paperwork. Even before it was completed, the Water Reclamation Facility was a major factor for several large corporations considering sites for expansion.

Even more important is what the development of the Water Reclamation Facility reveals about the way things work in Kalamazoo County. For more than a decade, concerned members of the community worked side-by-side with representatives from industry, government, and public interest groups to design, plan, and implement a wastewater treatment system capable of restoring the river as a source of community pride. The project was, as one official put it, "a model for the cooperation of public and private sectors."

The Water Reclamation Facility sits less than a mile from the spot where the first trading post was erected, on the oxbow of the river. Now, as then, Kalamazoo County beckons as a good place to live and do business.

Part

2

Kalamazoo County's Enterprises

Photo by John D. Strauss

W. KALAMAZOO
STUART

Kalamazoo County's energy, communication, and transportation providers keep products, information, and power circulating inside and outside the area.

94

Photo by Charlene Faris

WKZO Radio/Fetzer Broadcasting Service, 95

Kalamazoo Gazette, 96

Consumers Power/CMS Energy Corporation, 97

WKZO RADIO/FETZER BROADCASTING SERVICE

Radio was in its infancy in 1923, when young John Fetzer built his first radio station, WEMC, in Berrien Springs. Times were tough in 1931 when he moved it to Kalamazoo, taking the WKZO call letters from the city's name. The little 500-watt station doubled its power in 1936, broadcasting on the 590 frequency day and night. In keeping with its obligation to serve the public interest, WKZO increased its power to 5,000 watts full time as a regional clear-channel station by 1942.

Carl Lee joined the station as an

cal, regional, and national news and information with the area's largest radio news staff. The station continues a long tradition of daily farm broadcasts, offering market news and information tailored to the region. WKZO Radio carries the complete Detroit Tigers' baseball schedule. University of Michigan football and basketball, Detroit Lions football, as well as local high school football and basketball tournament action, round out sports coverage.

Listeners can follow a variety of music, talk, and interview programs

where local issues get a thorough airing. The station uses the services of three staff meteorologists to provide up-to-the-minute weather information, broadcasting freeze warnings to fruit farmers, road conditions, school closings, and disaster information. WKZO Radio earned special commendations for its coverage of the 1980 tornado and the ice storm of 1985, when staff members put in 24-hour days to keep area listeners well informed.

Radio has come a long way since 1931, when John Fetzer and his wife ran the station single-handedly. In addition to WKZO-AM, Fetzer Broadcasting Service owns WKJF-AM and -FM stations in Cadillac/Traverse City, and the nation's most powerful FM station at 320,000 watts— WJFM Radio, Grand Rapids. The company also owns Muzak franchises in outstate Michigan. Today's equipment provides miraculous fidelity, and computers now play an ever present role in modern radio broadcasting. And southwest Michigan's oldest radio station continues to be "Your Information Station."

Southwest Michigan's oldest radio station, WKZO Radio, provides news, information, and entertainment to a 29-county listening area.

engineer in 1939, and he rose through the ranks to become president of the company. He became owner of the Fetzer radio stations and Muzi-Tronic services in 1985.

The firm moved its headquarters from the old Burdick Hotel to 590 West Maple Street in 1958, making the address the best known in Kalamazoo. WKZO Radio is a full-service station, providing news, information, and entertainment to a steadily growing audience. It serves a 29-county listening area in southwest Michigan, providing needed services to a loyal audience.

WKZO Radio places a heavy emphasis on news; with affiliations with CBS, Mutual, Michigan Farm, and the Great Lakes Radio Networks, WKZO provides comprehensive lo-

KALAMAZOO GAZETTE

Bronson Park, in the center of downtown Kalamazoo, is ringed by churches and city and county government buildings.

Kalamazoo County's oldest business booms along in the space age as it did before Michigan became a state. Halfway through its second century, the *Kalamazoo Gazette* meets its readers' needs like a good neighbor. Though early readers would hardly recognize today's news, some things, such as the familiar "Jottings" column, remain. So does the paper's commitment to Kalamazoo.

The *Gazette* first appeared in 1837, a slender, four-page weekly. By the turn of the century 700 subscribers were reading its hand-set pages every day. F. Ford Rowe purchased the paper in 1899, installed modern linotype equipment, and increased circulation to 12,000 during his first seven years. Now part of Booth Newspapers, the *Gazette* reaches 162,000 adults in a six-county area.

Today's newspaper serves its readers in a variety of ways. It provides vital information on national and international happenings. It keeps its audience abreast of local news and consumer information. It allows readers to express their own opinions on issues of the day. Television brings the world into one's living room, but in fragments. Modern electronic printing and satellite communica-

tions give readers timely background on events and issues everywhere. More important, the *Gazette* gives readers a sense of community, covering local social and political issues, business, and sporting news. Entertainment sections announce activities; merchants put forth their offerings. Special correspondents regularly report from outlying areas. Publisher George Arwady says "People think of the *Gazette* as their newspaper, and they welcome it into their homes each day."

As the only daily paper published in Kalamazoo County, *Gazette* tries to present all sides fairly in its

news coverage and offers its readers a platform for their own ideas. Its opinion pages carry editorial comment, viewpoints from other papers, and a variety of syndicated columnists. A regular "Viewpoint" space features readers' comments, and the paper prints more than 2,000 letters to the editor each year.

Newspapers, like trusted advisers, offer insights on current issues and keep a community's memories as well. Nearly all of the thousands of *Gazettes* still survive, recording life in Kalamazoo. Ten decades ago Kalamazoo's first settlers looked to their paper once a week. Four pages carried all the young community's news and advertising. Today's *Gazette* calls on satellite news services, syndicated columnists, comic pages, supplements, crossword puzzle experts, reporters, and photographers. On any given Sunday it prints more than 80,000 papers filled with news and advertising, including almost 2,000 classified ads. According to Arwady, "The *Gazette* will be the area's leading news and advertising medium well into the next century."

One of the 10 oldest businesses in Michigan, the *Gazette* has a long tradition of service and of commitment to Kalamazoo's future. Since pioneer times it has measured the quality of life in a growing community, and, as Arwady says, "The *Gazette* tries to reflect that quality in its pages each day."

A tradition of service is carried on by the Kalamazoo Gazette from its headquarters at 401 South Burdick Street.

CONSUMERS POWER/CMS ENERGY CORPORATION

Frederick Bush organized the Kalamazoo Electric Company in 1886 to supply his neighbors' limited power needs. When his inefficient system proved inadequate, William A. Foote came from Jackson in 1898 to reorganize the company and to realize his dream of better service.

Few people really understood electricity then, and men such as Foote surmounted great difficulties through trial and error. Foote astonished electrical engineers in 1898 when he began the biggest earth-moving project ever seen in Michigan. He would dam the Kalamazoo River near Allegan and send 20,000 volts of electric current along iron wires to Kalamazoo, 24 miles away. It had never been done before. When the test came one year later, no one knew what the experiment would bring. After two hours, a rider galloped to the Trowbridge Dam shouting, "The lights is workin'!"

Foote succeeded better than he knew. He soon ran a second, 40,000-volt line to Allegan and on to Battle Creek and Jackson. In 1910 W.A. Foote pooled his resources with other electrical pioneers in the holding company he called Consumers Power.

Few of today's appliances existed in 1910, and few factories used electric power or natural gas. Since the 1850s Kalamazoo and Jackson had

been manufacturing gas from coal and resins in local plants, and in 1931 the company made the switch to natural gas discovered in Michigan. Ten years later Consumers met the massive demands by connecting with huge pipelines delivering gas from Louisiana and the Southwest. By 1949 Consumers carried electric power to its 100,000th Michigan farm, a feat no other utility has ever equalled. In the 1950s and 1960s Consumers added 19 big generating plants statewide. The company's newest generating plant, near Holland, was honored as the fifth most efficient coal-burning unit in the country. In the most recent national rankings, Consumers was found to be operating the most efficient generating plant system in the United States.

W.A. Foote knew that success

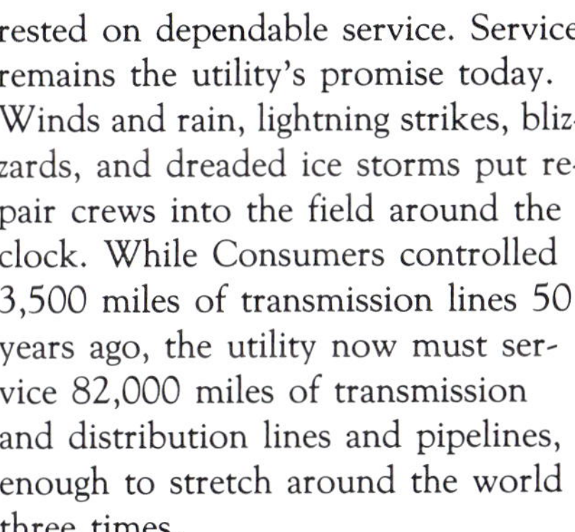

The J.H. Campell Plant, located in Port Sheldon Township, Ottawa County, has a capacity of 1,344 megawatts, enough power for a city of about one million people.

rested on dependable service. Service remains the utility's promise today. Winds and rain, lightning strikes, blizzards, and dreaded ice storms put repair crews into the field around the clock. While Consumers controlled 3,500 miles of transmission lines 50 years ago, the utility now must service 82,000 miles of transmission and distribution lines and pipelines, enough to stretch around the world three times.

Consumers continues to develop strategies to guarantee its customers' energy needs into the next century, so that whenever they throw the switch, "the lights is workin'!"

Consumers long ago recognized that its future would be linked to community growth. Today the quality of life depends on corporate citizens; Consumers spent $54 million during 1987 on environmental protection measures, and, by converting to low-sulfur coal, the firm completed a 13-year program to reduce emissions nearly 65 percent. The utility is now experimenting with new ways to turn coal ash into useful topsoil. Whatever the new century brings, Consumers Power continues its record of powering Michigan's progress.

The Hardy Dam, on the Muskegon River, is the largest conventional hydro plant on the Consumers Power Company system. It was completed in 1931 at a cost of $5.29 million and has a capacity of 30 megawatts, enough power for a city with a population around 24,000.

Producing goods for individuals and industry, manufacturing firms provide employment for many Kalamazoo County residents.

98

Photo by John Gilroy Photography

Green Bay Packaging/ Kalamazoo Container Division, 99

Clausing Industrial Inc., Startrite, Inc., 600 Group Incorporated, 100-101

Ship-Pac, Inc., 102

Precision Heat Treating, 103

General Motors—Kalamazoo Manufacturing Division, 104

Durametallic Corporation, 105

The Upjohn Company, 106

Fabri-Kal Corporation, 107

GREEN BAY PACKAGING/ KALAMAZOO CONTAINER DIVISION

thro
mer
pan
Grc
tior
trial
char
late

buil
tor
dus
U.S
ciat
thar
bro
por
fror
zil,
Anc
hist
dus
peri

A C
trolle

"There's no secret to making boxes," says Larry Murphy, president of Green Bay Packaging's Kalamazoo Container Division. How then does a local company grow to a $30-million business in a highly competitive industry? "You've got to do what you agree to do every time," Murphy believes. The ability to deliver a specific quantity of quality boxes on a daily basis—even at specific times of day—"that's what built this company."

Local paperman David Howard founded the company in 1953. Green Bay Packaging, which held a 50-percent equity, purchased Howard's interest in 1964. Since that time the Kalamazoo Container Division has been a wholly owned subsidiary of America's largest privately held corrugated-paper company. As such, the division met the two greatest challenges in the container industry: just-in-time delivery and point-of-purchase packaging.

More and more customers cut expenses and inventory by asking suppliers to deliver on a regular basis. With "just in time," failure to deliver quantity or quality containers halted the customer's own production. New technology, computerized labor-saving machinery, and around-the-clock operation increased the division's capacity, but human resources proved just as important.

The Kalamazoo Container Division is a subsidiary of Green Bay Packaging, America's largest privately held corrugated paper company.

The firm's 155 employees average 20 years' experience. Very little turnover and months without lost-time accidents showed that people took their work seriously. To help them be error-free on the job, the company introduced its Green Bay Quality Process in 1986. Adapted from Phil Crosby, the 14-step process involved everyone in the division and became part of the corporate culture. "It's in place, and it works," says Murphy. Old and new customers appreciate the effort. Just in time means customers must trust single-source suppliers to meet agreed-upon requirements, and the division's list of longtime customers is a measure of their success.

As retailers encourage self service, manufacturers find that packaging is largely responsible for selling their products. In a sprawling, state-of-the-art studio, company designers working with the latest CAD system provide customers with everything from concepts to actual tooling blue prints of the latest solutions to their individual packaging requirements. Boxes now must answer purchasers' questions and show them how to assemble and use a wide variety of items. Point-of-purchase packaging must appeal to buyers' needs and distinguish products from their competitors—no easy task.

Corrugated paper boxes may not be glamorous, but they protect and promote most of the things we buy. Green Bay Packaging runs a fully integrated system, harvesting the trees to make the paper, turning the paper into packages, and recycling any waste produced. The division uses no hazardous materials and keeps its operation environmentally sound. Lawrence Murphy calls the firm a service organization helping area businesses move their products. Employees know it as a good place to work. Customers find it a trustworthy supplier, and townspeople recognize Kalamazoo Container Division as an old friend.

New technology, computerized labor-saving machinery, around-the-clock operation, and a dedicated work force have made it possible to deliver quantity and quality containers on time all the time.

SHIP-PAC, INC.

In 1964 John and Margaret Vander Ploeg started Ship-Pac with $7,000 in a rented two-story house at Howard and Westnedge. They hoped to offer something that was unavailable anywhere in the state—one-stop shopping for shipping room supplies, packaging supplies, and packaging equipment.

The Vander Ploegs did everything themselves for the first year, even shoring up floor joists when their first big order proved too

Careful planning meant working conditions as up to date and efficient as any in the industry. Rooftop skylights flooded the modern office space with sunlight. Seven acres provided room for a new production area and a larger warehouse in 1985.

After 25 years John and Margaret remain active. Many of the responsibilities, however, now fall to daughter Kathie and sons Randy and Mike. Mike was born in the same year as the company, 1964. Kathie

John and Margaret Vander Ploeg founded Ship-Pac, Inc., in 1964 and are still actively involved.

"Everything You Need to Package Everything You Ship" is the Ship-Pac slogan. The modern office, production building, and warehouse are located in Kalamazoo's Covington Road industrial area.

heavy. Local firms gave them business, and suppliers offered their expertise as well as their inventory. A local bank provided financing, and in 1967 they moved to a new 6,000-square-foot-building that housed the company until 1980. That year Ship-Pac looked to the Covington Road industrial area, building and equipping a 24,000-square-foot-plant for $750,000. Kalamazoo's Economic Development Corporation assisted with revenue bonds.

played a major role in expanding Ship-Pac's Indiana market through the Elkhart office, opened in 1985. Seven years ago the firm began manufacturing some of its own products; Dow Chemical Co. granted one of only 13 licenses to make its protective foam nuggets. Randy designed an automated production system that Dow representatives call the most sophisticated they have seen. Aggressively marketed under Ship-Pac's own label as Fluffies®, the peanut-like, flowable packaging material sold at the rate of more than 240,000 cubic feet per month. Both the Elkhart office and the production division have fueled dramatic expansion in re-

cent years.

Ship-Pac's logo reads, "Everything You Need to Package Everything You Ship." The firm offers end products, equipment, consultation, and service for customers that need help with palletizing, protective packaging, carton closing, and marking. Products include plastic and steel strapping, stretch and shrink film, blister packaging equipment, mailing bags, gummed tapes, staples, poly bags, and tubing.

Ship-Pac, Inc., offers so many packaging aids that consultation is one of the company's most valuable services. Customer Audits suggest methods and products to help customers maximize economy and efficiency. Specialists service all types of packaging equipment, assisting a major cereal manufacturer, for example, with installing computerized ink-jet printers to encode its cartons.

John and Margaret Vander Ploeg once worked alone, but their family of 60 employees now helps them do more than $13 million worth of business annually.

PRECISION HEAT TREATING

Sprawling auto plants intimidated many Detroit newcomers, but not Wojciech Juzwiak. Trained as a blacksmith in Poland, Juzwiak understood metal. In particular, he knew what heat could do to enhance its properties. Sharpening his knowledge of production heat treating in the city's auto plants, Juzwiak joined others of his family in Kalamazoo, where he founded Precision Heat Treating in 1948.

Juzwiak's son, Roman, began to learn the business while he was still in grade school. When his father died in 1956, Roman stepped in to run the firm at 19. In the next quarter-century he made 10 additions to the plant, installing four more furnaces and adding sophisticated support equipment. Roman passed away in 1980, but his widow, Mary Jeanne, and sons, Donald, Paul, and Joe, con-

tinued the family tradition.

After 40 years in business, any company might rest on its accomplishments, but Precision doubled its plant capacity in 1987 and plans to increase again by one-third in 1988. Furnaces run continuously now, tended around the clock. The firm's top five customers, and many others, regularly repeat their orders, and two trucks travel daily pickup and delivery routes through southwest Michigan and northern Indiana. Precision has come to meet a real need among smaller and mid-size firms, which require sophisticated heat treatment but have no facilities of their own. The operation handles 5,000- to 10,000-pound orders efficiently, and meets special requirements for larger or smaller orders as well.

Great balls of flame roll toward ceiling vents as the furnace doors open. Firebrick interiors glow. Waves of heat shimmer around the machinery. Metal products line

Mary Jeanne Juzwiak (seated), president, and sons (from left) Donald, Joseph, and Paul carry on the family business, Precision Heat Treating, which was established in 1948.

heavy trays—products that enter the furnaces with one set of properties and come out with another, behaving differently even though they look unchanged.

Precision turned to computer monitoring in 1983. Shop manager Bill Call installed more than 100 special treating programs. Another computer tests for hardness, replacing interpretation with a swift and simple readout. Yet, for Call, the magic of blacksmithing still remains, as special orders and smaller jobs call for skilled hands.

Precision offers production heat treating, carbonitriding, and carburizing for a variety of area industries. The company can also treat any type of tool and die steel now in use, including stainless steel in surgical instruments and allied services. Specially designed induction heat-treating facilities offer great flexibility for specialized work, including silver, copper, and soft solder brazing. Precision's own machinery provides flame hardening for gears up to 36 inches in diameter, as well as for other parts.

This close-knit family company has kept pace with ever-increasing customer and community concerns. Precision Heat Treating uses no toxic materials and produces no toxic wastes. The company hopes to continue its enviable record and to expand its market as new industries move into the area.

Todd Burlingham carburizes a part while shop manager William Call checks the process.

GENERAL MOTORS—
KALAMAZOO MANUFACTURING DIVISION

Pioneer stagecoach driver J.G. Pattison would hardly recognize his Comstock farmland today. Imagine a 50-acre frontier farm, now under a single roof, with ceilings higher than the tallest barn he had ever seen. In it are 200 presses, some as big as a three-story building, pounding out steel body parts for automobiles that travel further in minutes than his stagecoach could in a day. But woodblock flooring still absorbs the heaviest loads, and "Do It Right the First Time!" makes as much sense as it might have a century ago. Today's General Motors fabricating plant com-

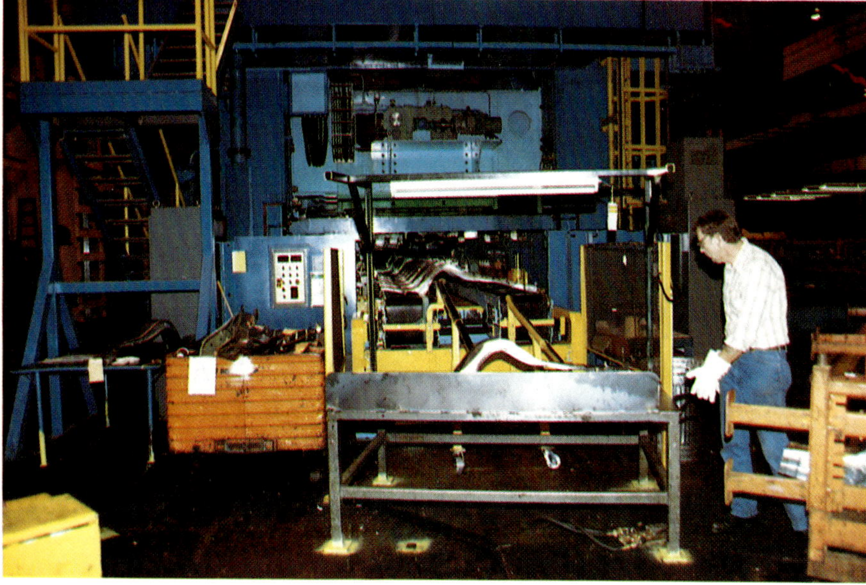

Above: A coordinate measuring machine is used to ensure the quality of the tools made in General Motors' modernized tool room.

Left: Giant transfer press technology provides greater productivity.

bines the most modern technology with old-fashioned quality and craftsmanship.

Seventy percent of the nation's auto business originates within 300 miles of Kalamazoo. Two hundred railroad cars and 225 just-in-time trucks leave the plant every week headed for assembly facilities throughout the region, as well as to GM operations in Canada, Mexico, and overseas. Opened in 1965, the facility employs 3,400 people and converts 1,300 tons of steel into car parts daily. The 2,000,000-square-foot operation is a bustling community in its own right, where workers use 200 electric carts, forklifts, and even bicycles to travel from one area to another. The company operates

its own school system for employees and provides a plant hospital equipped with the most modern medical and surgical facilities, including X-ray equipment. Continually upgrading, the plant now operates its own metallurgy laboratory. Its tool and die activity makes it a leader in the field of innovative technology, building the dies that will shape tomorrow's automobiles.

Just-in-time delivery has revolutionized American manufacturing. GM assembly plants depend on immediate delivery of quality stampings; the Kalamazoo plant keeps just five days ahead on orders. Skilled millwrights, electricians, and pipefitters must keep equipment humming. The company's Quality Control Division

is the nerve center of the operation, while digital electronic automation and robotics improve the metal-handling capabilities of the giant presses. Finished parts are monitored in the Green Room, where special lighting and sophisticated measuring devices detect any wavering from world-class quality.

Error-free production depends on clean dies and well-tuned machinery, but it also depends on craftsmanship. The company's Learning Center gives up-to-date instruction in production skills, and the Green Room provides a laboratory where employees absorb the firm's philosophy of continuous improvement. According to one prominent poster, "Our Next Inspectors are the Customers!"

Michigan's pioneers cleared the forests slowly; what they did, they did to last. Such care and attention to quality still have a place in today's world. The times may be different, but pioneers are much the same. People indeed continue to make the difference at this General Motors plant, where a poster on the wall proclaims, "Together we have the Answer."

DURAMETALLIC CORPORATION

What do paper mills, power plants, petroleum refineries, and chemical processing plants all have in common? They all rely on highly engineered machinery to process large volumes of liquids under a wide range of pressures and temperatures. One of the leading manufacturers of the sealing systems for this equipment is Durametallic Corporation of Kalamazoo.

Founded in 1917, Durametallic was the first U.S. manufacturer to recognize the immense potential of the mechanical seal, commit resources to developing it as a commercial product, and cultivate awareness of the technology in the marketplace. Over the years the company has introduced many of the major innovations in mechanical sealing technology.

In the modern 71,000-square-foot manufacturing center, workers begin with high-alloy steel bar stock. Using state-of-the-art equipment, including the most modern CNC computer-controlled machine tools, each seal is built to tolerances of as little as 33 millionths of an inch.

Today the firm operates seven manufacturing facilities in the United States and a total of 18 worldwide. In addition, Durametallic has more than 100 sales offices in 47 countries, including 60 in North America. Led by its highly respected Dura Seal line, Durametallic products are also available through a growing network of more than 60 authorized distributors.

The company's wholly owned subsidiary, Metal Fab Corporation in Ormond Beach, Florida, supplies metal bellows components for the Dura

This modern facility in Kalamazoo is the headquarters for Durametallic Corporation's worldwide sales and manufacturing network.

Seal line, as well as standard and custom-welded metal bellows devices for other high-technology, nonseal applications, such as the aerospace and medical fields.

Known for its high-performance products and worldwide marketing and support services, Durametallic is also a research leader in sealing design. Its R.D. Hall Research Center—located at the corporation's Kalamazoo headquarters—combines theoretical and practical research and state-of-the-art CAD technology in one of the finest facilities of its kind in the world.

Having recently completed the largest expansion project ever undertaken by the organization, Durametallic is prepared to meet the new challenges of the 1990s. The $3-million project, finished in 1989, doubled the space of the R.D. Hall Research Center and significantly expanded the firm's Marketing/Customer Service and Engineering de-

partments. In the past two years the company has increased its engineering staff by 33 percent and enhanced its already extensive CAD/CAM capabilities. In the future, the firm is planning to add CAD/CAM systems to its foreign affiliate offices to implement the system worldwide.

The company's current management team, headed by chairman, president/chief executive officer James S. Ware, a grandson of one of the founders, continues the philosophies and practices that have been so successful in the past: quality products at the lowest possible costs, comprehensive customer-support services,

The assortment of Dura Seal designs shown here illustrates the wide variety of configurations and sizes that are available.

and a genuine commitment to employee and environmental safety.

Durametallic enters the new decade well positioned to improve its market strength. With its new capabilities and longtime dedication to excellence and responsiveness to its customers, the company will keep the wheels of other industries turning for years to come.

THE UPJOHN COMPANY

Kalamazoo's largest employer began in an attic workshop more than a century ago. Today The Upjohn Company does $2.7 billion worth of business in 150 countries and employs 21,000 people worldwide—8,400 in Kalamazoo. It contributes roughly one billion dollars annually to the local economy.

Founder W.E. Upjohn found a better way to offer medication. For years he advertised the "friable pill" under his famous thumb. Medical practice changed dramatically in the twentieth century; 1,000 compounds came and went in company catalogs in the firm's first 75 years. The Upjohn Company prospered under its founder's guideline—"Keep the Quality Up."

In 1913 Upjohn brought in chemist Dr. Frederick Heyl to oversee product research and development. The company introduced proprietary products such as Cheracol cough syrup in 1924. Upjohn researchers combined kaolin clay with fruit pectin; they called it Kaopectate in 1936. During World War II Upjohn scientists learned to sterilize sulfanilamide powders; the firm produced almost 600 million of the famous wound tablets. Experimenting brought one new product after another, including a dramatic breakthrough in cortisone production that established Upjohn as the leader in the steroid field. Mo-

Upjohn's main pharmaceutical manufacturing plant in Portage contains more than 1.6 million square feet of floor space.

trin sales made pharmaceutical history in 1974.

In 1976 the company opened a new $43-million research and development center in Kalamazoo. Upjohn spends $300 million or more each year on research alone. Company scientists explore recombinant DNA possibilities on the cutting edge of the "biotechnology revolution." As board chairman Dr. Theodore Cooper puts it, "Research is high risk, but it's the future of the company."

The firm has pioneered ways to speed production, improve quality control, and lower costs. In 1951 experts nationwide looked to Building 41, the new 33-acre production facility on Portage Road (then the industry's largest under a single roof). Three years later the company began to place other manufacturing plants and research facilities worldwide. But Upjohn never lost touch with Kalamazoo County. In 1986 two-thirds of its capital expenditure, $135 million, went to local expansion, including the new Rogaine production

facility on East Kilgore Road.

In 1931 W.E. Upjohn purchased 1,262 acres near Richland to help feed the community's unemployed. He called helping neighbors "the most important thing I ever did." This effort grew into the $400-million Upjohn Agricultural Division, helping to feed people worldwide. Upjohn Healthcare Services is one of the nation's largest home health care organizations with offices in more than 200 cities and 60,000 workers. Since 1980 Upjohn has spent more than $266 million to ensure environmental quality of life for its workers and neighbors.

Cooper believes "The Upjohn Company and the Kalamazoo County community have grown up together." Employees and company alike return time and money to community projects. Celebrating its centennial, the firm announced a $2-million endowment to establish a Kalamazoo Area Mathematics and Science Center, offering special instruction to 300 area high school students. In 1988 The Upjohn Company made available a $10-million, five-year gift for community improvement.

Now in its second century, The Upjohn Company continues to make important contributions to health care and to community needs. As Cooper puts it, "We are proud of our headquarters community and look forward to continuing a strong, mutually beneficial relationship."

Brook Lodge, Upjohn's corporate conference center near Augusta, Michigan, was once the summer retreat of founder Dr. W.E. Upjohn.

FABRI-KAL CORPORATION

The modern, triangular corporate headquarters of Fabri-Kal Corporation overlooks the old Monarch Mill Pond, which was used by the paper industry more than a century ago.

Fabri-Kal's new corporate headquarters sits high on a hillside overlooking the old Monarch Mill Pond. Situated on 22 acres of woods and water in the heart of Kalamazoo, it is a showplace for the high-tech plastics industry. Designed for expansion, with full computer capability already wired, the 24,000-square-foot triangular building is intended to meet the company's needs for the next decade and become the center of a research and development campus.

Americans were just beginning to recognize the plastics revolution when Robert Kittredge, who specialized in plastic packaging for food and beverages, organized Fabri-Kal in 1950. As people came to expect more and better plastic containers, Fabri-Kal added faster equipment and a broader range of products for the food, beverage, dairy, pharmaceutical, and institutional markets. Now one of the largest thermoform specialists in the country, with sales of $85 million annually, Fabri-Kal uses its production facilities at Kalamazoo; Hazleton, Pennsylvania; and Greenville, South Carolina, 24 hours a day, seven days a week. In a year's time the company's 700 employees produce a staggering 8 billion items. Computers monitor production and quality; plastic trimmings are recycled. The firm's leadership in microwaveable packaging, individual juice cups, and fast-food restaurant containers and lids fueled major plant expan-

sions in 1986 and 1987.

Fabri-Kal designers specialize in custom products precisely tailored to customer needs; often such custom designs speed production and save energy. In addition, the firm developed tooling for hundreds of time-proven, low-cost stock cups, lids, and containers—clear, translucent, or colored. A substantial investment in equipment, research, and development gives fast turnaround time and better and more versatile material blends. State-of-the-art extrusion/forming machines provide

50,000-pound-per-hour capacity and can produce 40 million items daily. A Quality Assurance Program ensures fastidious care, even when orders run to millions of thermo-formed products. A process-oriented company, Fabri-Kal makes long-term staff and facility commitments—from blueprints, to tooling, to prototypes, to final production runs, and all the revisions in between.

Kalamazoo has been a central location for Fabri-Kal. The new headquarters and refurbished Cork Street plant will last a long time. "Our roots are here," says Kittredge, who urges reinvestment in the community. Through the years he has been a director of the First America Banks, and has headed the Rotary Club and the local and state chambers of commerce. He has also served as chairman of the 2,000-member Society of the Plastics Industry, and as a trustee for Kalamazoo College and the Lakeside Home.

The works of local artists hang on the skylighted walls of Fabri-Kal Corporation's headquarters. The century-old Mill Pond no longer serves the paper industry but reflects the dream of the future that Kittredge began to shape four decades ago.

The directors' boardroom at Fabri-Kal, with its spectacular view of the countryside.

Business and Professions

Kalamazoo County's business and professional community brings a wealth of service, ability, and insight to the area.

108

Photo by John Gilroy Photography

Kalamazoo County Chamber of Commerce, 109

Howard & Howard, 110-111

Pension and Group Services, Inc., 112-113

Old Kent Bank of Kalamazoo, 114-115

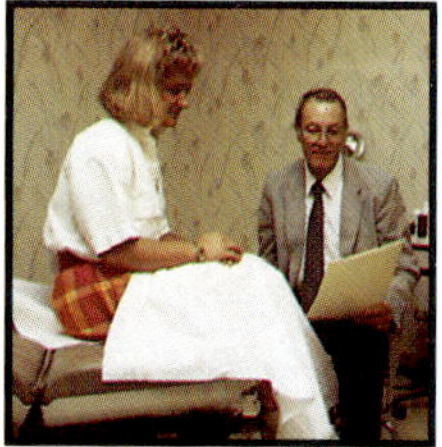

Physicians Health Plan, 116

Gilmore Enterprises Corporation, 117

Kal-Aero, Inc., 118

Superior Colour Graphics, 119

NBD Kalamazoo, 120

KALAMAZOO COUNTY CHAMBER OF COMMERCE

The Kalamazoo County Chamber of Commerce was founded in 1904 by a group of local business leaders who took it upon themselves to ensure that the community they were helping to shape and prosper would continue to grow into an area full of opportunity and hope for its citizens. They knew that only by working together for what they visualized —and working hard at it—could their Kalamazoo become a community with a high quality of life for all.

In the first few decades after its inception, those leaders and others worked through the chamber of commerce to help propel Kalamazoo from infancy to maturity. Simple but necessary issues such as establishing new roads and a traffic system that made sense, raising the money necessary to establish and support two of the five colleges and universities, establishing a community foundation—now the fourth largest in the nation, and creating the forerunner of today's United Way were priorities for this young organization and community.

Today, 85 years later, the community is "established," you might say, and its needs have changed. Because of its flexibility as a membership organization, the Kalamazoo County Chamber of Commerce has been able to keep up with change and reflect the needs of a growing society.

The organization's focus is the quality of its community, and its members share that vision. Working together the chamber's members believe it is possible to accomplish what none of us can do individually. The chamber's broad business constituency permits it to bring the vitality and expertise of the area's business community to bear on significant local issues.

As the voice for business in Kalamazoo County, the chamber of commerce works to maintain a favorable environment and quality of life for its business and professional members, as well as the community. Its primary efforts continue to be directed toward assisting business to

Kalamazoo County Chamber of Commerce has been working for 85 years to establish Kalamazoo County as an important trade center.

grow and prosper. The chamber helps expand investments and job opportunities that add to the economic activity in Kalamazoo County, and strives for excellence in services and programs offered to its membership and community.

From a young community at the turn of the century to a bustling cosmopolitan area of more than 200,000 people, the Kalamazoo Chamber of Commerce has watched its county grow. And it is proud to say it has helped shape Kalamazoo into the quality community it is today.

HOWARD & HOWARD

The phone rings 1,200 times per day at Kalamazoo's oldest and fastest-growing law firm. The Civil War had scarcely ended when William G. Howard began his practice in 1869. His son, Harry, joined him in 1899 and Harry's sons, William and John, entered the firm in 1929 and 1935, respectively.

Today Dick Howard represents the fourth generation to carry on the high-quality legal services William G. began. Keeping pace with an expanding economy and an increasingly complex legal system, Howard & Howard has grown phenomenally in the past few years, from seven staff attorneys in 1981 to more than 60 lawyers who today meet the needs of more than 2,000 clients statewide.

Now a major law firm in Michigan with offices in Bloomfield Hills, Kalamazoo, and Lansing, Howard & Howard expanded in part to assist its longtime clients that were growing rapidly themselves. The firm also recognized that specialization would allow it to service both old and new clients more efficiently. Large enough to offer expertise in specialty areas, Howard & Howard is at the same time small enough to give immediate, direct service tailored to individual needs.

In a tradition of personal service dating back to the beginning of the firm, each client has a principal attorney; but today this attorney may draw on the special skills of four or five colleagues. Howard & Howard provides a full array of business and corporate legal services, including advice and counsel concerning finance, securities, mergers, and international transactions. In addition, the firm has an extensive municipal law practice and represents a number of financial institutions. Recently the firm has expanded its government regulation practice, particularly in the areas of environmental law and telecommunications regulation. Labor, real estate, and tax law, and general litigation round out Howard & Howard's areas of practice.

J. Michael Kemp, managing partner.

Specialization also gives the organization's attorneys opportunities to develop new fields. Public interest in sweepstakes, coupons, and games of chance spurred the firm to develop a special field in promotional law. Firm attorneys trained themselves in cable television and computer law as well.

As a full-service law firm, Howard & Howard's staff members pro-

From left (seated) are John C. Howard, Richard J. Howard, and William J. Howard. William and John are the grandsons of the firm's founder and joined their father, Harry C. Howard, in the practice of law in 1929 and 1935, respectively. Richard is standing next to his father, William Howard, and is the great-grandson of the firm's founder.

vide its attorneys with the most sophisticated support available, including the area's largest and most complete law library. An in-house computer accesses case law from federal and state courts, and the public files of the Federal Register and the Securities and Exchange Commission. The firm's LEXIS system also provides access to international law libraries and an accounting library. In addition, the computer can summon the text of all stories appearing in ma-

jor newspapers and wire services during the past three years.

Managing partner Michael Kemp recruits new members with "fire in their belly," and encourages them to strengthen their particular fields and to seek out new business. Young attorneys have the benefit of more experienced mentors, and daily training, development, and counseling sharpens skills and contributes to long-range personnel goals. Working as a team, Howard & Howard can respond to complex legal problems that no single attorney could hope to unravel. "None of us has a monopoly on wisdom or judgment," says Kemp, "but together we do." Clients have come to expect timely service, and the Howard & Howard approach helps them maximize their abil-

prov
to m

prof
bene
pror
trust
tativ
vise
The
mak

emp
Buil

ity to achieve their objectives.

The firm works hard to keep clients aware of changing regulations. In addition to seminars and workshops, it publishes monthly legal updates that contain brief notices prepared by members suggesting strategies on a variety of issues. Readers may be advised on corporate record keeping, insurance planning, and copyright protection, and be informed of newsworthy national and international developments. In fast-moving areas such as cable television and environmental and promotional law, the

Howard & Howard has as one of its mottos: "We work hard and we play hard." This is evidenced by the fact that the firm is a two-time champion of the Greater Kalamazoo Corporate Olympics (1987 and 1988).

hist
ern
ting
of k
ers
in c
befc
P&
star
sult
esta
con
nies
that
thei

mo
tan
me
des
rec
tive
the

firm tries to alert clients before problems develop.

Michael Kemp believes that a law firm's responsibilities reach beyond courtroom and client. He encourages members to recognize the firm's long-standing role in community affairs. For example, he is a director of First of America Bank Corporation and of the Western Michigan University Foundation, where he also serves as an adjunct professor of government regulations and

Howard & Howard occupies four floors of The Kalamazoo Building, a fixture in the central business district since 1908, in downtown Kalamazoo.

business. He has worked with the chamber of commerce and headed the 1988 United Way Campaign. Howard & Howard sponsors a prestigious, $20,000, four-year Medallion Scholarship at Western Michigan University and supports a variety of community projects.

Any successful firm must balance the efforts of its staff and the needs of its clients. Howard & Howard works hard to maintain staff morale and involvement with the management process. Members make their success a firm success. "Our future," says Kemp, "depends upon our teamwork." That future seems bright. The rapidly growing offices in Bloomfield Hills and Lansing sug-

gest further expansion throughout the state.

Whatever the future may hold, Kalamazoo's oldest and largest law firm will certainly be a part of it. Howard & Howard's philosophy of "superior legal services in a timely fashion at a reasonable price" has served it well in the past century and in this one, and will continue to do so in the next century. As managing partner Kemp says, with "people who have fire in their belly, energy, and enthusiasm, you can't help but be confident about the future."

PE

Mai
hea
the
far
the
and
ben
vol
Wh
to
sio
ter

and
div
me
adi
pro
est
era
10
the

clu
tra
acc
and
pro
mc

Chapter

12

Building Kalamazoo County

From concept to completion, Kalamazoo County's building industry shapes tomorrow's skyline.

122

Photo by John A. Lacko

SCI/Steelcon, Inc., 123

Dykstra and Company, 124-125

Consumers Sand and Gravel Company/ Consumers Concrete Corporation, 126

Parkview Hills, 127

SCI/STEELCON, INC.

What do Detroit's Cobo Hall and People Mover have in common with Wings Stadium, Western Michigan University's Dalton Fine Arts Building, and the Three Rivers automotive plant? SCI/Steelcon, Inc., played an important role in all of these projects.

SCI/Steelcon, Inc., was founded in 1972. The company has grown from a handful of men working out of pickup trucks to one of the six largest steel erecting firms in the country. Computers in Kalamazoo and branch offices in Auburn Hills and Fremont, California, monitor projects nationwide. In the fast-moving construction world, the $30-million company has contracted with European, Far Eastern, and North American joint ventures.

Expanding rapidly during the past eight years, particularly in the automobile industry, SCI/Steelcon now operates four principal divisions: machinery installation, structural steel, precast concrete, and equipment rental. Such flexibility gives the firm a wide range of experience and counters the cycles that abound in construction work.

Beginning with the automotive plant in Three Rivers, SCI/Steelcon has helped construct and modernize facilities for the big three auto makers nationwide. The Machinery Installation Division assists in model changeover, retooling, and robot applications. This division allows the company to specialize in complete turnkey plant assembly and automated machinery systems coast to coast. SCI/Steelcon is responsible for the electrical, painting, piping, conveyors, oven systems, and miscellaneous equipment that makes modern factories hum.

Steel and precast concrete construction depends on heavy equipment far too expensive for many contractors. Steelcon makes available its own equipment on a rental basis and can provide everything from forklifts to cranes. The firm's crane fleet ranges from four- to 230-ton capacity, and its forklifts are able to lift machinery weighing up to 60,000 pounds.

SCI operates with the team approach in the construction field. Customer-contractor relationships are top priority in today's high-cost construction. The company manages entire projects from start to finish. Daily contact with customers, quick decision making, and efficient scheduling assure successful completion of projects. Coordination and cost control are high priority items at SCI. Computerized scheduling and experienced field personnel help to complete projects on time and within budget. Local and nationwide clients bring their business back many times over. SCI/Steelcon, a Kalamazoo-based company, is putting its mark on construction from the East Coast to the West and many places in between, and has the ability to meet clients' needs nationwide.

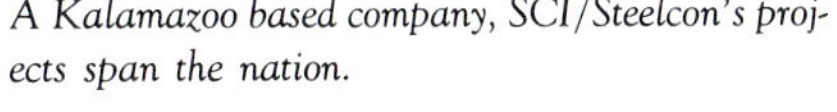

A Kalamazoo based company, SCI/Steelcon's projects span the nation.

SCI/Steelcon makes its own equipment available on a rental basis and can provide everything from forklifts to cranes.

CONSUMERS SAND AND GRAVEL COMPANY/ CONSUMERS CONCRETE CORPORATION

Joseph Lowe grew up knowing wooden sidewalks and streets paved with brick or cedar blocks. Turn-of-the-century builders laid up stone foundations and ordered local sand and gravel as it was needed. Lowe worked in paving and contracting for many years, organizing the Kalamazoo Construction Company in 1916. As residential construction grew along East Main in the 1920s Lowe opened a borrow pit on Nazareth Road to serve local needs.

The name, Consumers Sand and Gravel Company, was first used in the 1934 city directory. Brothers Adrian and Richard Klepper with a third partner, Richard Butcher, bought the business in 1938, and the company expanded throughout the community. In 1941 Adrian Klepper's son-in-law, Donald W. Thomas, joined the firm. With the passing of Richard Klepper and then Richard Butcher, the business was then perpetuated by the Adrian Klepper family.

Consumers Sand and Gravel Company incorporated in 1946. Donald W. Thomas became an officer in the firm eight years later. In 1976 the

One of Consumers' many modern delivery trucks ready for loading.

third generation assumed the management of the corporation. The four grandsons of Adrian Klepper and the sons of Donald W. Thomas became Consumers Sand and Gravel Company officers—Tom W., president; Stephen A., vice-president; Gregory A., secretary; and Donald B., treasurer.

One of the first to introduce transit mix concrete service in the area in the 1930s, Consumers has seen ready-to-pour concrete replace sand and gravel as its major emphasis. The "old firm with the new image" owns the largest fleet of front-discharge trucks in the state. Consumers has tripled its operation since 1984, now serving 10 counties with 12 regional plants. As the area's largest supplier, Consumers has provided concrete for many well-known buildings, industrial plants, college and university buildings, and residences.

High technology plays an important role in company strategy. The firm was the first to introduce two-way radios and six-wheel-drive, front-loading trucks to the area, and to build a state-of-the-art batch plant in 1981 that can supply as many as 30 trucks per hour. Sand and gravel passes to the batch plant by conveyor from a 350-ton-per-hour crushing plant nearby. Computer terminals monitor the batching process, programmed to provide up to 200 different mixes.

Consumers Concrete Corporation supplies concrete for both residential and commercial construction. The company's founders chose a site with extraordinary natural resources, and the new generation now plans confidently for the future on its sprawling complex stretching between Nazareth Road and Sprinkle.

The Kalamazoo location of the state-of-the-art ready-mix concrete batching facility.

PARKVIEW HILLS

Parkview Hills is a planned residential community dedicated to maintaining the integrity of the environment. The Kalamazoo Nature Center is a facility for educating thousands of people. Both of these places share a founder, Dr. H. Lewis Batts, Jr., and beautifully fulfill his concepts.

The Nature Center, established in 1961, interprets basic ecological principles and realistically demon-

Parkview Hills, a 288-acre planned unit development (PUD) on Kalamazoo's south side, has successfully demonstrated that ecological and aesthetic values need not be inconsistent with economic concerns.

strates the history of Michigan rural life. Parkview Hills broke ground in 1970 to, in Batts' words, "produce a state of harmony between people and the land" in modern urban life.

Believing that aesthetics need not be inconsistent with sound economics, Batts, an internationally known educator and ecologist, purchased a 288-acre tract of rolling, submarginal farmland on the south side of Kalamazoo. He joined with the late Burton H. Upjohn, who directed marketing and building, contributing his practical business savvy. Victor Gruen and Associates of New York (originator in the 1950s of the downtown mall) provided planning, and the city commission passed a Planned Unit Development ordinance to foster flexible zoning.

This was no ordinary construction project. Roads curved to existing terrain, bulldozers avoided

honeysuckle shrubs, and sewers circumvented oaks and flowed under pines. Dwelling lots platted on high ground permitted scenic views and served to preserve low spots with the best vegetation. Structures designed to be looked out of and not at were integrated into the natural environment.

The tract bordered two small natural lakes, Lime Kiln and Hill 'N' Brook. Little Portage Creek, an intermittent stream, was dredged and dammed to restore two other lakes, Cherry Creek and Willow. Traditionally, deep wells provided city water, but acres of blacktop and storm sewers channeling rainwater via the Kalamazoo River to Lake Michigan failed to replenish the aquifer. By maintaining a high water level on the two restored lakes, water percolated down through a sand layer while a runoff system that conducted storm water

to catch basins preserved a high percentage of the rainfall.

More than 100 acres are set aside as permanent open space, encompassing at least 20 feet around marshlands and waterways. Four miles of nature trails ramble through groves of wild cherry and oak trees, inviting hiking and cross-country skiing.

Stressing diversity, structures include a mixture of condominium town houses, apartments, and detached homes; rental apartments and town houses; and single-family homes, as well as three small office buildings, a 10-shop convenience square, a 200-seat restaurant, and a community clubhouse designed by a variety of architects. A wide range of prices brings corporate chief executive officers, professionals, newlyweds, retired persons, and clerical workers together, bound only by a common love of nature. Management and sales functions are exclusively offered by Greenleaf Realty, located in the original farmhouse on the site.

Batts, with Upjohn's help, has made Parkview Hills the successful expression of the Kalamazoo Nature Center vision.

Health and Education

Medical and educational institutions and museums and philanthropic foundations enrich the lives of Kalamazoo County residents.

128

Photo by John D. Strauss

Nazareth College in Kalamazoo, 129

Borgess Medical Center, 130

Bronson Healthcare Group, Inc., 131

Kalamazoo Valley Community College, 132

Kalamazoo Consortium for Higher Education, 133

Western Michigan University, 134-135

Kalamazoo College, 136

Kalamazoo Aviation History Museum, 137

A Community of Foundations, 138-139

NAZARETH COLLEGE IN KALAMAZOO

Standing straight and true for 64 years, the magnificent stone wall and entrance gate on Gull Road reflect the quality and care that Nazareth College brings to higher education. Founded in 1924 by the Sisters of St. Joseph, the coeducational college offers its 900 students a close-knit community and professors and staff who inspire self-discovery.

Over the years Nazareth has combined the liberal arts and sciences with professional preparation in 23 major programs of study that stress practical experience. Teacher Education students begin field work as early as their first year. Nursing students develop 30 percent more clinical experience than usually required, and the Nurses Independent Learning Center offers hands-on training in a lab equipped with modern professional equipment. Unique programs in Fine Arts Management and Pharmaceutical and Medical Services reflect current job markets.

At the graduate level, Nazareth offers a Master of Education degree. The Master of Arts in Management stresses the development of skills, knowledge, and attitudes needed for working effectively with people in a wide range of business settings.

In describing Nazareth's Agenda for Excellence, president Patrick Smith noted that the college "is committed to educating the whole person, intellectually, spiritually, socially, and physically." Students have access to support services for tutoring and counseling, and small classes and a low faculty/student ratio means greater personal attention. The David Metzger Library contains 96,000 volumes and subscribes to 500 periodicals. The new Nazareth College Sports Center provides students and the community with basketball, racquetball, track, and weight training facilities. Both students and staff encourage community involvement, coordinated by the director of Campus Ministry/Volunteer Services.

Nazareth serves the community in many ways. In addition to making

Above: The quality and care that Nazareth College brings to education is also reflected in the attractive landscaping surrounding the campus. Courtesy, John Gilroy Photography

Left: Students of all ages find value in the congenial atmosphere of Nazareth classes.

classes available to other college students, the school opens its library to the community and schedules events and workshops open to the public. It provides degree completion programs for community college graduates throughout southwest Michigan, and the Continuing Education Office offers working adults a variety of learning opportunities and credit for life experience. Growing numbers of these nontraditional students turn to off-campus continuing education classes, held at convenient evening and weekend hours.

Students find a comfortable yet challenging environment on the 59-acre campus, set on 150 acres of woods, fields, and ponds three miles north of downtown Kalamazoo. All buildings are centrally grouped and many are connected by tunnels, which gave rise to the campus mascot—the mole. Two residence halls accommodate 250 men and women. At Nazareth College, students achieve the basis for a lifetime of work as they learn the college motto: "Scholarship, Service, Opportunity."

BORGESS MEDICAL CENTER

Opened by 11 Sisters of St. Joseph in 1889, Borgess Hospital admitted four patients in its first six months. Today the 426-bed medical center and its 2,000 employees offer specialized care to thousands of area residents.

Kalamazoo's first hospital outgrew repeated additions to its original quarters on the corner of Portage and Lovell streets, and in 1917 a new and larger Borgess opened on 40 acres along Gull Road, just in time for the great influenza epidemic. Hospital care grew ever more sophisticated as the years passed, and hospital staff members introduced pioneering innovations. Dr. Homer Stryker developed the famous Stryker turning frame in 1936 and followed with other inventions, including a safety saw for cutting casts and the circ-o-lectric bed for traction patients. Dr. Richard Upjohn Light introduced the first outstate neurosurgical and neurological outpatient services in 1936.

Building on Dr. Light's beginning, Borgess now offers the region's most extensive program for neurological care, including one of Michigan's three Neuro Intensive Care Units and a new Spinal Injury Center, the first of its kind in the area. With the best of equipment and support personnel, neurosurgeons perform the complete spectrum of procedures, including microsurgery, laser surgery, ultrasound, and neurophysiologic monitoring.

Borgess Medical Center established southwest Michigan's only comprehensive open-heart surgery program in 1972, just five years after the first coronary bypass ever performed. Today the facility incorporates the most recent advances in heart care.

Modern hospital care reaches beyond initial treatment and techniques. Borgess Medical Center offers the area's only kidney transplant program, has opened satellite centers for kidney treatment, and trains dialysis patients to treat themselves. A comprehensive, multidisciplinary approach leads to preventive and rehabilitative programs such as the Institute for Cardiovascular Health and the Midwest Recovery Center for alcoholism. The DeLano Clinic offers Fitness for the Mind workshops and mental health services to a nine-county area.

Despite miracle drugs and mechanical apparatus, Borgess' mission, "to heal the sick," still depends on caring people. Compassion, love, and spiritual strength play their part in patient recovery. One of the first open-heart surgery patients in 1972, Bud Small, has been a Borgess security officer for 11 years. He visits heart patients on his nightly rounds, reassuring them with insights from his own experience. "If I can make a post-op patient smile," he says, "it makes my day."

Keeping up with revolutions in medical care, Borgess launched a three-year, $43-million construction and renovation program. Future health care needs will be even more complex than they are at present. Working together, health care specialists can sharpen their focus and integrate their skills in diagnosis, education, and prevention. As it enters its second century, Borgess Medical Center hopes to become the hospital of the future—today.

Embarking upon its second century, the 426-bed Borgess Medical Center still fulfills its original mission, "to heal the sick." The health care center is equipped with the latest state-of-the-art equipment and techniques and a compassionate and caring staff.

BRONSON HEALTHCARE GROUP, INC.

Bronson Healthcare Group, Inc., is parent to a comprehensive system of health care services in southwest Michigan. At the heart is Bronson Methodist Hospital in Kalamazoo, a 456-bed regional hospital founded in 1900. Bronson offers virtually every specialty and subspecialty in medicine and surgery.

Bronson Healthcare Group is also parent to Bronson Vicksburg Hospital, a 42-bed medical/surgical and rehabilitative facility, and Bronson Crosstown Center, which houses outpatient surgery, gerontology, adult day care, rehabilitation, and women's health services. Bronson Care Centers in Kalamazoo, Galesburg, and Plainwell provide healthy living

specialized care in Bronson's 45-bed Neonatal Intensive Care Unit.

The Bronson Health System for Women and Children also encompasses the largest pediatric unit and the only pediatric intensive care unit in the region. Bronson's Center for Women's Health provides outpatient gynecological and breast screening services, counseling, and education. ChildCare PLUS offers day and evening care; The Care Corner provides care for mildly ill children.

Trauma care is another Bronson specialty. Its regional Trauma and Emergency Center provides services for more than 41,000 patients every year, and the hospital's unique Trauma Care Unit offers a valuable

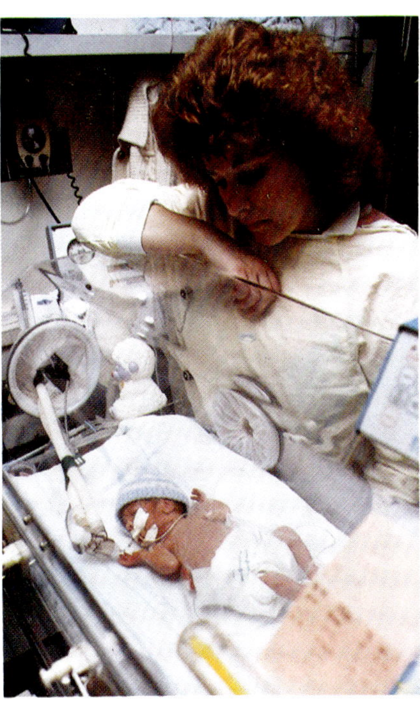

Bronson's Neonatology Program was established in 1972. Today at-risk newborns are referred to Bronson's Neonatal Intensive Care Unit from more than 20 regional hospitals.

A fixture in downtown Kalamazoo for nearly a century, Bronson Methodist Hospital provides high-quality health care for southwest Michigan.

environments for more than 260 nursing home residents.

Recognized as the regional leader in health care for women and children, Bronson delivers more than 3,100 babies every year. Bronson's regional Perinatal Center offers special care for at-risk mothers. At-risk newborns are transported to Bronson from hospitals throughout southern Michigan and northern Indiana for

continuum of care as trauma victims complete their recovery. Noteworthy, too, are the services of Bronson's 24-hour, in-house trauma surgeon.

Designated the region's Burn Center since 1973, the hospital also houses a Hyperbaric Oxygen Unit for victims of carbon monoxide poisoning, diving accidents, and related injuries. Bronson critical care transport services include a helicopter ambulance unit.

Bronson's new Center for Digestive Health and Disease was created

to address another hospital specialty, and senior citizens take advantage of many programs offered by Bronson's Older Adult Services. The Gerontology Center, Adult Day Care Center, and Bronson Care Centers are complemented by a respite care program and GoldenCare PLUS, a membership and counseling program. Bronson Place, a continuing care retirement center, will be completed in 1990.

Finally, Bronson provides education for patients, health care professionals, and area residents with programs sponsored by the Bronson Institute for Health Education and through HealthAnswers, a free telephone and walk-in information resource.

For nearly a century a growing network of Bronson services have been integrated to best serve the community's health care needs. Today Bronson Healthcare Group, Inc., continues to work toward its mission to be southwest Michigan's leader in diagnosis, treatment, and health education.

KALAMAZOO VALLEY COMMUNITY COLLEGE

In 1966 the electorate of the nine public school districts in the Kalamazoo Valley Intermediate School District overwhelmingly approved the establishment of Kalamazoo Valley Community College. In 1969 the Mattawan School District annexed to the KVCC District, making 10 public school districts that comprise the college's legal district.

Two decades later the college welcomes more than 20,000 students annually on 187 acres in the rolling hills of Texas Township and at the Downtown Center, opened in 1983. The modern campus is on a natural slope adjoining the Al Sabo Natureland Preserve. Today the college comprises more than 370,000 square feet and is currently in the process of a major facilities expansion.

Fully accredited by the prestigious North Central Association of Colleges and Schools, KVCC offers more than 55 programs leading to certificates and associate degrees. The current catalog lists 502 courses and more than 100 professional staff members. Some students turn programs into immediate employment while others transfer to four-year colleges and universities for the baccalaureate degree. Still others attend for enrichment purposes or participate in summer activities for schoolchildren ranging in age from seven to 17. KVCC presents so many opportunities in so many situations at so many sites that it is hard to see where the campus ends and the community begins. Credit or non-credit, degree programs or selected courses, daytime or evening, weekday or weekend, KVCC offers something for everyone.

An open admissions policy challenges every student to succeed, and challenges the college to provide the opportunity for them to succeed. Individual needs assessments and career counseling help focus students' aspirations, and small class size makes for more individualized contact with instructors and hands-on experience. The Learning Resources Center holds 70,000 volumes and 32,000 audiovisual items, including radio and television. Students may use the multimedia Learning Laboratory, tutoring services, and special support services, and the cooperative education program gives on-the-job training.

The average age of KVCC students is 30, many of whom come to the school with families and careers well established. The college schedules classes to accommodate people working full or part time, and recently introduced a structured-learning play center where students may leave their children during class hours.

Serving on the board of directors for the 1,200-member American Association of Junior and Community Colleges, KVCC president Marilyn Schlack keeps in touch with concerns nationwide and has helped Kalamazoo Valley Community College expand its role in community and economic development. Education for Employment, a countywide vocational education program; retraining; and lifelong learning courses now keep pace with students' career choices and general education programs. Personal and community needs have changed markedly in the past two decades, but the goal to serve those who want to succeed remains.

Kalamazoo Valley Community College welcomes 20,000 students annually at its Oshtemo Campus (above) and the Downtown Center (below).

KALAMAZOO CONSORTIUM FOR HIGHER EDUCATION

The term "college town" has special meaning for Kalamazoo, as the Kalamazoo Consortium for Higher Education has shown since its inception in 1973. Founded by the presidents of Kalamazoo College, Kalamazoo Valley Community College, Nazareth College, and Western Michigan University, and joined by Davenport College in 1983, the consortium maintains the diversity of its members while sharing programs, resources, and services.

Combined, the five schools employ more than 1,000 faculty and 2,000 staff, and reach some 35,000 students annually. Physical plant values total more than $325 million, and operating budgets amount to nearly $150 million yearly. The consortium offers the schools, students, and community a variety of benefits, and group purchases save thousands of dollars in supply money each year.

The Kalamazoo Consortium for Higher Education sponsors a computer network allowing its schools to share data sources, a system that, along with joint planning of programs and sharing of resources, allows each school to maintain its uniqueness and to serve the community in ways that are complementary rather than competitive. A recently inaugurated Inter-Institutional Studies Program allows students to enroll for classes at any member school while paying tuition at their own college rate. They may also share library and audiovisual resources. Legislative funding allows the consortium to sponsor special programs and ongoing research to meet community needs, including five new projects that got under way in the spring of 1988. In particular, the organization is tapping the expertise of its schools to assist the community and the region in the field of economic development.

The president's council meets regularly, and consortium leadership rotates from school to school. Working together, the member schools can provide for their own future while jointly strengthening institutional quality and services to students and the community.

Institutional variety is a key strength in the American system of higher education, but competition often brings expensive duplication. By combining the resources of the five schools to serve residents of the greater Kalamazoo community and beyond, the Kalamazoo Consortium for Higher Education offers a unique blend of educational, social, and cultural opportunity and has become a model for colleges in similar situations nationwide.

WESTERN MICHIGAN UNIVERSITY

Established in 1903, Western Michigan University has grown into a major university with a significant statewide role. One of the state's five graduate-intensive, research-oriented institutions, it is helping shape West Michigan's future through economic development and enhancing the quality of life. Western's first classes accommodated 117 students; today 24,500 pursue degrees in any of 220 programs.

The university's economic impact is estimated to be more than $334 million annually. The institution is governed by a board of trustees, comprised of eight distinguished citizens, appointed by the governor.

As a measure of intellectual excellence, Western invites more than 600 high school scholars to compete for its prestigious Medallion Scholarships. Among the largest in public education today, these $22,000 awards have been made possible by individuals, corporations, foundations, and other organizations that have put their faith in the university's commitment to education, research, and service.

The Medallion Scholars and other entering students find almost unlimited opportunities at WMU's seven academic colleges and three

The Friedman, Dunbar, and Knauss building complex with the familiar block W shrub in the foreground.

schools. They may pursue training in arts and sciences, business, education, engineering and applied sciences, fine arts, general studies, and health and human services, plus an interdisciplinary Honors College. Some turn to the schools of Music, Public Affairs and Administration, and Social Work. Through the years Western has developed nationally recognized centers of excellence in printing, rehabilitating the blind, psychology, speech pathology and audiology, occupational therapy, computer literacy, aviation, and medieval studies.

Students come from every county in Michigan, from other states, and from more than 70 foreign countries. One in three is nontraditional or over the age of 25. Student services range from intramural athletics to academic skills enhancement, plus intercollegiate athletics in the Mid-American Conference and other leagues. The Women's Center, the Office of Off-Campus Life, the University Counseling Center, and the Office of International Student Services suggest some of the opportunities open to students and the community alike.

The Graduate College enrolls 25 percent of Western's students, making it the fourth-largest program in the state. It offers 60 master's degrees and nine doctoral programs, including the only doctorate in public

Students enjoy spring and the weeping cherry trees in front of the Seibert Administration Building.

administration in Michigan. The Carnegie Foundation for the Advancement of Teaching designates WMU as Doctoral I, putting it in the company of schools such as Alabama, Boston College, Notre Dame, and Texas Tech.

Committed to regional education and economic development, Western began off-campus programs in 1905. Its Continuing Education Division, now the second largest in the state, serves more than 10,500 students annually through six regional centers. These regional centers provide 60 sites in nearly 30 communities with 25 complete degree programs and more than 200 courses each semester. In addition, an Office of Evening and Weekend Programs coordinates scheduling of 1,000 courses for adult, part-time, and evening students on campus. Project SCOPE helps senior citizens enroll in university classes free of charge.

A comprehensive university encourages research as well as teaching, and Western offers a wide variety of research incentives through its Office of Research and Sponsored Programs. The university's 770 faculty members attract more than $8 million in outside research grants—proposals have increased 72 percent, and outside support has doubled in

the past two years. The school provides a laboratory and computer support and a variety of other benefits. The Dwight B. Waldo Library holds in excess of 2.5 million items of printed, microform, and audio material. The library has an on-line computer for searching and access to the Center for Research Libraries in Chicago. One out of eight students uses the 15,000 linear feet of manuscripts housed in the university archives and regional history collections. The archives also serves some 5,500 community patrons each year.

According to president Diether Haenicke, "Western Michigan University reaches out to people all over Michigan." Residents of West Michigan may think first of 50,000-watt WMUK or the 3,500-seat Miller Auditorium, home of the Kalamazoo Symphony Orchestra. They may have taken part in WMU's many music and theater offerings, or sent their children to the Michigan Youth Arts Festival or other special learning opportunities.

Western participates in a variety of business-industry partnerships as well. The paper and printing science department pilot plants help industry test products and processes from tree to printed page. Through the state's Research Excellence and Economic Development Fund, Western operates the Applied Mechanics Institute, the Horticultural Economic Development Center, and the Water

Resources and Contaminant Hydrology Center. WESTOPS, Western's Office of Public Service, responds to 500 requests annually; the John E. Fetzer Business Development Center and the Business Research and Service Institute link school and community, offering management development programs, workshops, and specialized seminars; and the Small Business Institute allows teams of students to work as consultants to area firms.

Recognizing "the vastness of the knowledge still to be explored," Western is preparing for the next century. A physical renaissance will add a $17.1-million College of Business building and $5 million worth of improvements for paper and printing facilities. A $17-million renovation and addition to Dwight B. Waldo Library will be accompanied by a $7.6-million academic computer center. With a $9.3-million telecommunications system just installed, Western Michigan University is ready for the information revolution. It will continue "to introduce the student to the world in which the educated and responsible citizen must live."

Above: The Miller Auditorium fountain with Sprau Tower on Dalton Plaza in the background.

Below: East Hall, Western's first building, dates back to 1903.

KALAMAZOO COLLEGE

Kalamazoo College is nestled in a 60-acre wooded hillside in the heart of the city. One of the country's 100 oldest schools, it opened in 1833 when Michigan was still a territory. Over the years this highly selective liberal arts college blended a broad education and preprofessional training while placing special emphasis on the sciences. Eighty percent of the school's 1,250 students go on to graduate or professional study, achieving a phenomenal 96-percent acceptance rate at medical, dental, and law schools.

Such success depends on motivated students, distinguished faculty, and innovative programming. More than half of first-year students rank in the top 10 percent of their graduating class, bringing skill and enthusiasm to their studies. A light teaching load and a student/faculty ratio of 12 to one allow instructors to work with students individually and to introduce them to the newest research.

In 1962 Kalamazoo College introduced its unique "K" plan designed to enrich traditional learning with off-campus experiential education. Guided by faculty advisers, students move through a regular sequence of on-campus and off-campus semes-

Nestled in a 60-acre wooded hillside in the heart of the city, Kalamazoo College is one of the country's 100 oldest schools. A unique blend of tradition and innovation provides a challenging educational atmosphere at this highly accredited liberal arts college.

ters. They begin with a career development internship in the sophomore year. As juniors, 90 percent of the students will study and travel overseas for one or two terms; with help from a special endowment fund, they will pay only regular on-campus tuition for this experience. Finally, seniors work a full term on an individual project that they have chosen and developed. The "K" plan encourages confidence and independence by sharpening social and decision-making skills, and by offering students a wider perspective on the world around them.

Kalamazoo College has always prepared its students for the future and is now readying itself for the next century. New buildings include tennis, swimming, and athletic centers. Stetson Chapel, a community landmark, has been extensively renovated, as have all six dormitories, and a multimillion-dollar science complex

is in final planning stages. In addition to physical expansion, the college is moving academically. A new general education core introduces great intellectual and artistic achievements to students, regardless of curriculum. Strong African and expanded Asian studies programs, including language offerings, reflect today's shrinking world.

The college continues its service to the community as well. Its 300,000-volume Upjohn Library is a primary reference source. Its rare book collection has been a draw in the community for years. Nontraditional programs enrich and extend formal education to area residents, who may audit regular courses or attend special noncredit seminars. The Stryker Center for Management Studies and Educational Services helps public and private organizations develop their human resources and serves as the Small Business Development Center for Southwestern Michigan.

In the next century, as in the present one, Kalamazoo College will continue to offer its unique blend of tradition and innovation, of academic prestige and personal attention, and of support and challenge.

KALAMAZOO AVIATION HISTORY MUSEUM

on a Republic P-47D Thunderbolt. After disassembling the aircraft, they carefully clean airframes inside and out and recondition or replace defective parts. Rewiring follows, and, if necessary, fuselage and wings may be reskinned. After painting and engine overhauling, the aircraft emerge in better-than-new condition.

Such care has brought the museum nationwide attention, numerous awards, and six Grand

Left: Time stands still at the Kalamazoo Aviation History Museum, which houses one of the country's premier collections of 1940s aircraft.

Below: One of the massive aircraft engine exhibits at the Air Zoo—the Allison V-1710-111.

During World War II Americans built and flew nearly 300,000 planes. Most of these flying machines have succumbed to the ravages of a half-century. But time stands still at the Kalamazoo Aviation History Museum. Founded in 1977, it houses one of the country's premier collections of 1940s military aircraft. Its restoration program is internationally recognized, and 75 percent of its planes still fly regularly.

Redesigned and expanded in 1987, the nonprofit museum now attracts some 30,000 visitors, a figure expected to double in the next two to three years. Time slips away in a spotless, 47,000-square-foot display area, where piston-driven planes of another era stand ready to fly again. Visitors may clamber into a Link Trainer or climb aboard a Douglas C-53/DC-3. They file past an immaculate Cessna Bird Dog—"the jeep of the sky" to Marines who flew the unarmed spotter plane at treetop levels and highway speeds. There are the four Grumman "cats"—the Wildcat, the Bearcat, the Tigercat, and the famous Hellcat, which turned the tide in the Pacific. Everywhere in the main hangar stand the legends of military aviation, chiefly from World War II, though the collection includes aircraft that have participated in the Korean and Vietnam conflicts.

The museum offers a library and archives, a theater featuring period films, and a variety of educational displays. In 1988 the Guadalcanal Campaign Veterans' Association added its own special collection as well. Museum activities extend far beyond the hangar walls, with special programs bringing the experience to schoolchildren and staff pilots taking selected planes to special events throughout the eastern half of the country.

Executive director Robert Ellis feels a special responsibility to keep the legendary warbirds flying. New acquisitions go to the museum's restoration center, where staff members recently spent 10,000 hours working

Champion Warbird citations from the Experimental Aircraft Association at the nation's largest air show in Oshkosh, Wisconsin. Kalamazoo's Air Zoo is now one of the few places in the world where aviation history lives in special flight-of-the-day programs. As Ellis puts it, "It is in the sky that the grace and beauty of these remarkable machines intertwine with the skills of their pilots to come truly alive."

Kalamazoo's Air Zoo preserves the heritage of military aviation, not to glorify war, but to pay tribute to the men and women who designed, built, maintained, and flew some of the most extraordinary piston-driven aircraft the world has ever seen.

A COMMUNITY OF FOUNDATIONS

More than a century ago Henry Little stood at the Pioneer Society Picnic recounting the early days of Kalamazoo County. He talked of hospitality and generosity long before "ten-dollar boots and hundred-dollar dresses." Then, success amounted to clearing a little more land, providing food for the table, cash for taxes, and a little laid by each year for those in need. He remembered neighbors helping at barn raisings, quiltings, husking bees, and when families were hurt by sickness or fire.

thropy rose with the fortunes of the twentieth century. During the Progressive Era many wealthy families—Carnegie, Ford, Rockefeller, Rosenwald, Sage—established permanent endowments under professional management. Others pooled their resources in "Community Foundations." Today 30,000 private and public foundations, including 900 in Michigan, contribute $93 billion yearly in charitable gifts. More than a dozen local foundations perpetuate the legacy of Kalamazoo's early philanthropists.

The Sculptor's Stone *is a hallmark of the Kalamazoo Foundation. Photo by Concord Photo Labs*

The new Nazareth College Sports Center was built with the aid of a grant from the Kalamazoo Foundation. Photo by John Gilroy Photography

As the country grew and prospered, people began to think about the community. They supported churches and charities. Dr. Edwin Van Deusen gave liberally for the town's first library. Well-to-do families pledged funds for the Academy of Music Building and other civic improvements.

The Gilded Age after the Civil War built fortunes; responsibilities came with success. Andrew Carnegie rose from bobbin boy to one of America's richest people. In 1889 he reminded us in the prestigious *North American Review* that we were only stewards of our wealth, called upon to use it wisely. Sensible people should "give as much time and thought to dispensation of wealth as to accumulation."

America's interest in philan-

Dr. W.E. Upjohn met with community leaders one day in 1925 to offer $1,000 in seed money to create the Kalamazoo Foundation "for the mental, moral, and physical improvement of the inhabitants of the County of Kalamazoo." Townspeople helped the foundation expand. Donald Gilmore joined the board of directors in 1928 and served as president from 1934 to 1975. Under his guidance Kalamazoo Foundation grants reached $2 million annually.

Continually drawing new support, the Kalamazoo Foundation reported more than 700 gifts in a recent year. One of the oldest community foundations in the country, it is

now the 16th largest, with total assets of $62.3 million. In 1987 its directors disbursed nearly $6.5 million. As current president William J. Lawrence, Jr., puts it, "The Kalamazoo Foundation inherited its unique spirit of cooperation from this community's early philanthropists, and has been learning what it means to the residents of this community for more than 60 years."

Pioneers looked out for each other. Today three times the population of pioneer Michigan lives in Kalamazoo County alone. Maintaining the quality of life becomes ever more complex. Yet people continue to share their good fortune as they did in those simpler times. Most of Kalamazoo County's philanthropic foundations reflect the desires of individuals who hoped to make a difference.

Grace Upjohn established the Harold and Grace Upjohn Foundation in 1958 to promote "the alleviation of human suffering" and to "assist in the improvement of living, moral, and working conditions." With more than $5 million in assets, the foundation helps "specific charitable projects . . . which cannot be financed through the regular budget of eligible organizations." In its first quarter-century the foundation distributed some $3 million to almost 100

This enormous 10,000-piece pipe organ, which was handcrafted near Montreal, Quebec, was hand installed piece by piece in Kalamazoo College's Stetson Chapel, a purchase and project supported by the Gilmore Foundation. Pictured are Judith Breneman, Bach Festival director, and Paula Pugh Romanaux, the college organist.

local organizations, helping launch new projects, purchase specialized equipment, or meet sudden expenses.

Educated as a concert pianist at Yale, Irving Gilmore returned to take his place in the family merchandising business in 1925. He lived a frugal, watchful life, marking the changes of modern times and helping others when he could. Retiring from active management in 1971, he established a foundation to carry on his vision of service. When he died in 1986, the bulk of his estate went to the foundation, which held assets of $85 million at the end of 1987. The trustees approved 129 grants totaling almost $7 million in 1986 and 1987. In accordance with Irving Gilmore's instructions, the foundation encourages applications from greater Kalamazoo for projects in the performing arts, human services, health and

well-being, education, and youth and community development.

John E. Fetzer grew up with crystal sets and mastered the air waves in the early days of broadcasting. He came to Kalamazoo in 1930, determined to bring radio service to the community. Over the years he continued to pioneer, first in radio, then in television. By 1962 he also solely owned the Detroit Tigers. Yet, like other pioneers, Fetzer preferred to "keep moving ahead to new things and new challenges." He established the John E. Fetzer Foundation in the 1950s. In the 1980s he turned his

holdings into a $193-million endowment to "support research, education, and service, especially in the high-risk areas on the frontiers of knowledge, science, and the spirit."

A 57,000-square-foot 21st Century Center in the woodlands of Oshtemo Township offers futuristic working conditions for 30 staff members. It can also serve as an international communications and teleconferencing center. The large computer system can provide "a worldwide data base for frontier sciences," networking researchers and practitioners in the physical, mental, and spiritual health fields.

Believing "that a healthy, whole, positive, and productive person is the first step toward a healthy,

global community," the Fetzer Foundation convened a global conference in 1988 on "Helping Heal the Whole Person and the Whole World." Some 850 conferees found themselves, as foundation president Dr. Glenn Olds put it, on "the cutting edge of what we know and what we do." Perhaps John Fetzer best described the foundation's aim when he said, "We are exploring the unknown."

Businessman Jim Gilmore once noted, "Every generation breeds a few men and women who challenge the rest of us to look beyond what

The John E. Fetzer Foundation headquarters is nestled in the woodlands of Oshtemo Township, west of the city of Kalamazoo. Photo by Arcadia, Kalamazoo

is now." Those men and women who established Kalamazoo's public and private foundations left a legacy of "generous wisdom from the past, supporting us in the present, and preparing us for the future." According to the Kalamazoo Foundation, "It is a legacy as permanent as a granite boulder, yet as flexible as the changing times." Like the first pioneers, our foundations remind us that old-fashioned precepts still have value, that people need to look out for each other, and that "neighbors helping neighbors" can make a better world for us all.

Patrons

The following individuals, companies, and organizations have made a valuable commitment to the quality of this publication. Windsor Publications and the Kalamazoo County Chamber of Commerce gratefully acknowledge their participation in *Kalamazoo County: Where Quality Is a Way of Life.*

Borgess Medical Center*
Bronson Healthcare Group, Inc.*
Cain Realtors
Clausing Industrial Inc.
   Startrite, Inc.
   600 Group Incorporated*
A Community of Foundations*
Consumers Power/CMS Energy Corporation*
Consumers Sand and Gravel Company/Consumers Concrete Corporation*
Durametallic Corporation*
Dykstra and Company*
Fabri-Kal Corporation*
General Motors—Kalamazoo Manufacturing Division*
Gilmore Enterprises Corporation*
Green Bay Packaging/Kalamazoo Container Division*
Howard & Howard*

Kal-Aero, Inc.*
Kalamazoo Aviation History Museum*
Kalamazoo College*
Kalamazoo Consortium for Higher Education*
Kalamazoo Gazette*
Kalamazoo Valley Community College*
National Flavor Products
Nazareth College in Kalamazoo*
NBD Kalamazoo*
Old Kent Bank of Kalamazoo*
Parkview Hills*
Pension and Group Services, Inc.*
Physicians Health Plan*
Precision Heat Treating*
SCI/Steelcon, Inc.*
Ship-Pac, Inc.*
Superior Colour Graphics*
The Upjohn Company*
Western Michigan University*
Wilkins & Wheaton Engineering Corp.
WKZO Radio/Fetzer Broadcasting Service*

*Participants in Part II, "Kalamazoo County's Enterprises." The stories of these companies and organizations appear in chapters 9 through 13, beginning on page 94.

Select Bibliography

An Art Center Grows in the Midwest, 1924-1961. Kalamazoo Institute of Arts, 1966.

Arts Council of Greater Kalamazoo, 1986 Annual Report. Arts Council of Greater Kalamazoo, 1986.

Ayres, Raymond. *Highlights in Galesburg History.* N.p., 1919.

Bennett, Andrew. *Development of the Kalamazoo Public Schools, 1900-1914.* Kalamazoo College, 1956.

Bennett, Samuel V. *Industrial Land Supply in the Kalamazoo Area.* W.E. Upjohn Institute for Community Research, 1949.

Borgess Magazine. Borgess Medical Center, 1987.

Comstock Bicentennial. Comstock Bicentennial Committee, 1976.

Dunbar, Willis. *Kalamazoo and How It Grew.* School of Graduate Studies, Western Michigan University, 1969.

Early Days of Augusta. N.p., n.d.

Fennell, Vivian. *Scotts—Past and Present.* N.p., n.d.

Griffith, Lester. *Gull Lake.* N.p., 1964.

History of Kalamazoo County, Michigan. Evarts Publishers, 1880.

Hodgman, F.R. *Early Days in Climax.* N.p., 1905.

Houvener, Helen E. *How Dear to Our Hearts: Augusta, 1776-1976.* N.p., 1976.

Kalamazoo. Kalamazoo County Chamber of Commerce, 1982.

Kalamazoo County Connection. Kalamazoo County Chamber of Commerce, 1987.

Kalamazoo Valley Consortium/Education for Employment, Annual Report, 1986-1987. Kalamazoo Valley Intermediate School District, 1987.

Kalamazoo Valley Intermediate School District Plan for the Delivery of Special Education Programs and Services, 1988-1989. Kalamazoo Valley Intermediate School District, 1988.

Kekic, Nick. *A Fine Place for a City: Titus Bronson and the Founding of Kalamazoo.* Oak Opening Press, 1984.

Living Here. Weekly supplement to the *Kalamazoo Gazette,* July 19, 1987.

Massie, Larry B., and Schmitt, Peter J. *Kalamazoo: The Place Behind the Products.* Windsor Publications, 1981.

McKean, Eugene C.; Harrison, Marjorie M.; and McBridge, Carol C. *Richland: From Its Prairie Beginnings.* Richland Community Library, 1981.

McTaggart, Fred. *Water for Tomorrow: A Community Commitment.* Kalamazoo Water Reclamation Plant, 1982.

Molineaux, Grace. *Water Over the Dam: Vicksburg Then and Now.* Vicksburg Historical Society, 1972.

Phillipps, D. *Galesburg Area Centennial: 1869-1969.* Kal-Gale Printing Co., n.d.

Potts, Grace J. *Portage and Its Past.* Edited by Posie Tomlinson. Portage Public Schools, the City of Portage Public Library, 1976.

Skinner, Helen. *The Prairie Celebrates Our Nation's Bicentennial in Schoolcraft, Michigan.* N.p., 1976.

Vicksburg: A Physical Improvement Program. Prepared by the Village of Vicksburg, Vicksburg Foundation, by Wilbur Smith and Associates, n.d.

Index

GENERAL INDEX

Italicized entries indicate illustrations.